A SHORT HISTORY OF MAN

The Mises Institute dedicates this volume to all of its generous donors and wishes to thank these Patrons, in particular:

Adam J. Bagby
Douglas E. French and Deanna L. Forbush
Jing Jin and Wai Chan
Charles and Anne-Lisbeth Sebrell
Elijah Joel Smith
John Tate

Anonymous
John Bartel
Richard Beverly Bleiberg
Herbert Borbe
Jorge Carlos Borlandelli Zeballos
Mary E. Braum
Dietmar Georg
Hunter Hastings
Albert L. Hillman, Jr.
Richard J. Kossmann, MD
David Kramer
Arthur L. Loeb
The Morgan Report
R. Nelson and Mary Nash
Jorge Roca Arteta
Morten Rustad
Reginald Thatcher
Joseph Vierra
William Vinck

A SHORT HISTORY OF MAN

PROGRESS AND DECLINE

AN AUSTRO-LIBERTARIAN RECONSTRUCTION

HANS-HERMANN HOPPE

MISESINSTITUTE

"On the Origin of Private Property and the Family" and "From the Malthusian Trap" first appeared in Hans-Hermann Hoppe, *The Great Fiction: Property, Economy, Society, and the Politics of Decline* (2012); reprinted with permission of Laissez Books (Baltimore, Maryland).

"From Aristocracy to Monarchy to Democracy" was published as a booklet by the Mises Institute (2014).

Cover design by Chad Parish featuring ancient cooking and storage pots and the historical and ancient beehive houses in Şanlıurfa, Turkey.

Mises Institute
518 West Magnolia Avenue
Auburn, Alabama 36832
mises.org

ISBN: 978-1-61016-591-4

To

Gülçin

CONTENTS

Foreword by Llewellyn H. Rockwell, Jr. 9

Introduction:
An Austro-Libertarian Reconstruction 13

1. On the Origin of Private Property
and the Family 21

2. From the Malthusian Trap to the Industrial
Revolution: Reflections on Social Evolution 73

3. From Aristocracy to Monarchy to Democracy 103

Index 133

About the Author 141

FOREWORD

Hans-Hermann Hoppe is one of the most remarkable libertarian scholars of our time. He began as a prize student of Jürgen Habermas, the famous German philosopher and social theorist. Habermas was, and remains to this day, a committed Marxist. He is the leader of the notorious Frankfurt school.

Habermas was very impressed with Hans, and, under the patronage of this eminent Marxist, Hans had every reason to expect a stellar academic career in his native Germany. A problem soon arose, though, one which has had happy results for all those who love liberty. Hans soon came to realize that the leftism and socialism he had grown up with was intellectually barren and morally bankrupt. He discovered on his own the great works of Ludwig von Mises and Murray N. Rothbard.

Austrian economics and Murray's anarchism were not what Habermas had in mind. By becoming a libertarian, Hans effectively ended his chances for a chair at a major German university, even though his intellectual accomplishments easily qualified him for one. Like Murray, though, Hans is a scholar of complete intellectual integrity. He would not surrender what he had come to realize was the truth, whatever the cost to his own career.

Hans decided to come to United States in order to study with Murray, who was then teaching in New York. When I met him, I was struck by Hans's firm commitment to Rothbardian principles and his outstanding intellectual ability. Murray, of course, immediately grasped Hans's potential. When Murray was named to an endowed chair in economics at the University of Nevada, Las Vegas, he worked to get Hans a position in the economics department as well. Together, the two of them made UNLV a major center for the study of Austrian economics; and they did so in the face of much opposition from some of their departmental colleagues.

Murray was especially intrigued by one of Hans's main arguments. Hans's teacher Habermas pioneered an approach to ethics based on the conditions for engaging in rational argument. In a way that Habermas would hardly approve, Hans turned Habermas's ethics on its head. Instead of support for socialism, argumentation ethics as Hans explained it provided powerful support for self-ownership and private property. Murray heartily approved and highly praised Hans's argument:

> Hans Hoppe has ... deduced an anarcho-Lockean rights ethic from self-evident axioms. Not only that: he has demonstrated that, just like the action axiom itself, it is impossible to deny or disagree with the anarcho-Lockean rights ethic without falling immediately into self-contradiction and self-refutation. (*Liberty*, November 1988)

Hans had reversed Habermas; but not content with this, he again overturned conventional opinion. Like Murray, Hans is an anarcho-capitalist. The best government is no government at all. The question nevertheless arises: in a world of states, what type of government is the least bad? Almost everybody says "democracy." Unfortunately, many libertarians agree. Hans showed in his classic *Democracy: The God That Failed* that democracy leads to profligate spending and reckless policies. Those in power know that they will remain in charge only for a limited time. Their attitude will be "get all you can and get it now." By contrast, a king will tend to be less exploitative. He will try to preserve the lives and property of his subjects, because he is no temporary ruler, and wants to pass on a prosperous kingdom to his heirs. Hans of course did not say that monarchy was a "good thing," just that it tends to be better than democracy. The great Catholic classical liberal Erik von Kuehnelt-Leddihn, who had influenced Hans, said this was a brilliant insight.

"From Aristocracy to Monarchy to Democracy," one of the essays included in *A Short History of Man*, summarizes Hans's position. Readers of this scintillating work will discover that if monarchy is better than democracy, aristocracy is better still. If you haven't read Hans before, you have a treat in store for you. In just a few pages, he will make you question everything you have ever read about government.

Throughout *A Short History of Man*, Hans shows how the lessons of Austrian economics can be used to help us understand history. In doing so, Hans is following the path laid down by his great mentor, Murray Rothbard. Like Murray, Hans is a scholar of near universal interests. He is fully at home in anthropology and sociology, as well as global history, economics, and philosophy.

Drawing on his vast knowledge and Austrian insights, Hans addresses two questions. How did the family and private property originate? How did the Industrial Revolution get started? Readers will see how the development of secure property rights and the free market has been essential to human progress. The question for our times then is: Will these developments continue, to the great benefit of mankind, or will the state be able to thwart them?

In its use of economics and philosophy to illuminate history, *A Short History of Man* brings to mind such libertarian classics as Oppenheimer's *The State*, Nock's *Our Enemy the State*, and Chodorov's *The Rise and Fall of Society*. *A Short History of Man* is an ideal introduction to the thought of a major social thinker and outstanding libertarian.

— Llewellyn H. Rockwell, Jr.

INTRODUCTION: AN AUSTRO-LIBERTARIAN RECONSTRUCTION

The following studies try to explain three of the most momentous events in the history of mankind.

First, I explain the origin of private property, and in particular of ground land, and of the family and the family household as the institutional foundations of agriculture and agrarian life that began some 11,000 years ago, with the Neolithic Revolution in the Fertile Crescent of the Near-East, and that has since — until well through the late nineteenth century — come to shape and leave an imprint on human life everywhere.

Second, I explain the origin of the Industrial Revolution that set off around 1800, only some 200 years ago in England. Until then and for thousands of years, mankind had lived under Malthusian conditions. Population growth was constantly encroaching on the available means of subsistence. Every productivity increase was "eaten up" quickly by an expanding population size such that real incomes for the overwhelming bulk of the population were held down constantly near subsistence level. Only for about two centuries now has man been able to achieve population growth *combined* with *increasing* per capita incomes.

And third, I explain the parallel origin and development of the *State* as a territorial monopolist of ultimate decision-making, i.e., an institution vested with the power to *legislate* and *tax* the inhabitants of a territory, and its transformation from a monarchic State, with "absolute" kings, to a democratic State with "absolute" people, as it has come to the fore in the course of the twentieth century.

While this could suffice as an introduction and the reader could proceed directly to the following chapters, a few additional remarks may be in order for the philosophically minded reader.

Until the early twentieth century, the following would have been classified as *sociological* studies. But with the rise and increasingly dominant influence attained in the course of the twentieth century by the empiricist-positivist-falsificationist philosophy, the term *sociology* in the meantime has acquired a very different meaning. According to the empiricist philosophy, normative questions — questions of justice, of "right" and "wrong" — are not scientific questions at all — and consequently most of modern, "scientific" sociology, then, is dogmatically committed to some variant of *ethical relativism* (of 'anything goes'). And the empiricist philosophy categorically rules out the existence of any non-hypothetical, non-falsifiable, or synthetic a priori laws and truths — and accordingly modern sociology is dogmatically committed also to some variant of *empirical relativism* (of 'everything is possible,' of 'you can never be sure of anything,' and 'nothing can be ruled out from the outset').

My studies are and do everything a "good empiricist" is not supposed to be or do; for I consider the empiricist-positivist philosophy wrong and unscientific and regard its influence especially on the social sciences as an unmitigated intellectual disaster.

It is demonstrably false that ethics is not a science, and that no universal principles of justice exist and no "true" (non-arbitrary) criterion of distinguishing moral progress from decline. And it is likewise demonstrably false that no universal and invariant laws of human action and interaction exist, i.e., no laws of what is and is not possible and of what can and cannot be successfully done in human affairs, and no non-arbitrary criterion of judging actions as correct and successful or incorrect and faulty solutions to a given problem or purpose.

As for the second, 'positive' claim, it is contradicted by the entire body of Classical Economics. Classical Economics, reconstructed, refined, and further advanced during the "Marginalist Revolution," in particular by its Viennese branch, founded by Carl Menger (1840–1921) with his *Principles of Economics* (1871) and culminating with Ludwig von Mises (1881–1973) and his unsurpassed *Human Action* (1940), and by what has since become known as *Austrian economics*, provides the intellectual material for a grand, comprehensive system of non-hypothetically true laws of human action, of *praxeology* — the logic of action — and of praxeological laws.

Any explanation of historical events must take praxeology — and specifically Ludwig von Mises — into account, and it is the "empiricists" who are insufficiently empirical in their work. In denying or ignoring the underlying praxeological invariants and constants in their observations of the social world, they fail to see the forest for the trees.

And as for the first, 'normative' claim, it is contradicted by the entire body of private law, in particular the law of property and contract, that grew up in response to the continued occurrence of interpersonal conflict regarding scarce resources. From the old 'natural law' tradition of the Stoics, through Roman law, to Scholastic law, to the modern, secular 'natural rights' tradition, a body of law and of scholarly literature on matters of law had emerged by the nineteenth century, that should put any ethical relativist to shame.

Buried for a long time under mountains of positivist legal rubbish, this tradition has been rescued and reinvigorated, refined, and rigorously reconstructed in our time above all by Murray N. Rothbard (1926–1995), most notably in his *Ethics of Liberty* (1981), to the until now most comprehensive system of natural law and the political philosophy of *libertarianism*. Any normative evaluation of historical events and developments that aspires to the rank of science, i.e., that claims to be more than an arbitrary expression of taste, must take account of libertarianism, and of Murray Rothbard in particular.

Hence, to indicate the *method* guiding my studies in the history of man, the subtitle of my little book: *An Austro-Libertarian Reconstruction.*

The events in human history that I want to explain are not necessary and predetermined, but *contingent empirical* events, and my studies then are not exercises in economic or libertarian theory. They will have to tell history as it really was and take account of all known facts. In this regard, I do not claim any originality. I do not unearth any unknown facts or dispute any established findings. I rely on what others have established as the known facts. But the facts and the chronology of events do not contain their own explanation or interpretation. What distinguishes my studies is the fact that they explain and interpret the history of man from the conceptual vantage point of *Austro-Libertarianism*: with the background knowledge of praxeology (economics) and of libertarianism (ethics). They are conducted in awareness of the non-hypothetical or aprioristic character of the laws of praxeology and of ethics and the fact that such laws impose strict logical limitations on what — which one — explanation or interpretation, of all conceivable explanations and interpretations of some given historical data set, can be considered at all *possible* and *possibly (hypothetically) true* (and so be scientifically admissible), and which ones can and must be ruled out instead as *impossible* and *impossibly true*. History, then, is *rationally reconstructed*, i.e., with the knowledge that every possibly true empirical explanation and interpretation must be in accordance not only with the 'data' but in particular also with praxeological and ethical laws, and that every explanation or interpretation at variance with such laws, even if apparently 'fitting the data,' is not only empirically false but not a scientifically admissible explanation or interpretation at all.

The history so reconstructed and retold is to a significant extent *revisionist history*, opposed not only to much or even most of what the dominant leftist "mainstream" has to say on the matter, but, owing to the emphasis placed in my studies on human inequalities and in particular on unequal cognitive abilities and psychic dispositions, opposed also to much pronounced and proclaimed in this regard by some circles of "politically correct" and "progressive" so-called "cosmopolitan" establishment-libertarians.

Thus the first momentous event in the history of man, the Neolithic Revolution, is reconstructed as a cognitive achievement of the first order and a great progressive step in the evolution of human intelligence. The institution of private land ownership and of the family and the practice of agriculture and animal husbandry is explained as a rational invention, a new and innovative solution to the problem faced by tribal hunters and gatherers of balancing population growth and increasing land scarcity.

Similarly, the Industrial Revolution is reconstructed as another great leap forward in the development of human rationality. The problem of balancing land and population size that had been temporarily solved with the original invention and subsequent spread and worldwide imitation of agriculture had to eventually re-emerge. As long as the population size increased, per capita incomes could be increased only if and for as long as productivity increases outstripped population growth. But steady productivity increases, i.e., the continuous invention of new or more efficient tools for the production of ever more, new or better products, requires a continuously high level of human intelligence, of ingenuity, patience, and inventiveness. Wherever, and as long as such a high level of intelligence is lacking, population growth must lead to lower — and not to higher — per capita incomes. The Industrial Revolution, then, marks the point, when the level of human rationality had reached a level high enough to make the escape from Malthusianism possible. And the escape is reconstructed as the result of the "breeding," over many generations, of a more intelligent population. Higher intelligence translated into greater economic success, and greater economic success combined with selective marriage- and family-policies translated into greater reproductive success (the production of a larger number of surviving descendants).

This combined with the laws of human genetics and civil inheritance produced over time a more intelligent, ingenious and innovative population.

Lastly, while the Neolithic and Industrial Revolutions are reconstructed as correct and innovative solutions to a persistent problem: of a population size encroaching on living standards, and hence as great intellectual advances, the third momentous event to be explained is the invention of the State. The State is a territorial monopolist of ultimate decision-making and its successive transformation from a monarchic to a democratic State, is reconstructed as the outcome of a sequence of cumulative intellectual — moral and economic — errors and as a step back in the development of human rationality and a growing threat to the achievements attained with the Industrial Revolution. *Per* construction, the State *cannot* achieve what it is supposed to achieve. It is supposed to produce justice, i.e., to uphold and enforce the law, but with the power to *legislate* the State can — and inevitably will — *break* the law and *make* law in its own favor and so produce instead injustice and moral corruption. And the State is supposed to protect the property of its subjects from foreign invasion, but with the power to *tax* its subjects it can — and inevitably will — expropriate the property of these subjects not, obviously enough, to protect *them* and their property, but to 'protect' *itself* and its expropriations against any so-called "invader," foreign or domestic. As an "expropriating property protector," i.e., as a fundamentally "parasitic" institution, the State can never help but will always *hinder* in the production of wealth and so *lower* per capita incomes.

In combination, then, with the following studies I hope to make a small contribution to the old tradition of grand social theory and render the long course of human history from its very beginnings to the present age more intelligible.

Hans-Hermann Hoppe
Istanbul, January 2015

1

ON THE ORIGIN OF PRIVATE PROPERTY AND THE FAMILY

I. THE SETTING: HISTORY

IT IS REASONABLE TO BEGIN HUMAN HISTORY five million years ago, when the human line of evolutionary descent separated from that of our closest nonhuman relative, the chimpanzee. It is also reasonable to begin it 2.5 million years ago, with the first appearance of *homo habilis*; or 200,000 years ago, when the first representative of "anatomically modern man" made its appearance; or 100,000 years ago, when the anatomically modern man had become the standard human form. Instead, I want to begin only 50,000 years ago, when "anatomically modern man" had evolved into "behaviorally modern man." This is an eminently reasonable starting point, too.[1]

"Behaviorally modern human" refers to the existence of hunter-gatherers, of which even today some small pockets

[1]See on the following Nicholas Wade, *Before the Dawn* (New York: Penguin Press, 2006).

have remained. Based on archeological evidence, humans living 100,000 years ago were apparently still largely inept at hunting. They were certainly unable to take down large and dangerous animals, and it appears that they did not know how to fish. Their tools were almost exclusively made of stone and wood and made of materials of local origin, indicating the absence of any distance travel or trading. In distinct contrast, about 50,000 years later the human toolkit took on a new, greatly advanced appearance. Other materials were used besides stone and wood: bone, antler, ivory, teeth, shells, and the materials often came from distant places. The tools, including knives, needles, barbed points, pins, borers and blades were more complex and skillfully crafted. The missile technology was much improved and indicated highly developed hunting skills (although bows were invented only about 20,000 years ago). As well, man knew how to fish and was apparently able to build boats. Moreover, next to plain, functional tools, seemingly purely artistic implements: ornaments, figurines and musical instruments, such as bird-bone flutes, appeared on the scene at this time.

It has been hypothesized that what made this momentous development possible was a genetic change leading to the emergence of language, which involved a radical improvement in man's ability to learn and innovate. The archaic humans — *homo ergaster*, *homo neanderthalensis*, *homo erectus* — did not have command of a language. To be sure, it can be safely assumed that they employed, as do many of the higher animals, the two so-called lower functions of language: the expressive or symptomatic function and the trigger or signal function.[2] However, they were apparently incapable of performing the two higher, cognitive functions of language: the descriptive and especially the argumentative function. These unique human abilities — so uniquely human indeed that one cannot think them 'away' from our existence without falling into internal contradictions — of forming simple descriptive statements (propositions) such as "this (subject) is 'a' (predicate)," which claim to be *true*, and especially of presenting arguments (chains of propositions) such as "this is 'a'; every 'a' is 'b'; hence, this is 'b'," which claim to be *valid*, emerged apparently only about 50,000 years ago.[3]

Without language, human coordination had to occur *via* instincts, of which humans possess very few, or by means of physical direction or manipulation; and learning had to be either through imitation or by means of internal (implicit) inferences. In distinct contrast, with language — that is with words: sounds associated with and logically tied to certain objects and concepts (characteristics) — coordination could be achieved by mere symbols; and learning thus became independent of sense impressions (observations) and inferences could be made externally (explicitly) and hence became

---

[2]On the "lower" and "higher" functions of language see Karl Buehler, *Sprachtheorie. Die Darstellungsfunktion der Sprache* (Stuttgart: UTB, 1982; originally published in 1934); and in particular also Karl R. Popper, *Conjectures and Refutations* (London: Routledge, 1963), pp. 134f., and idem, *Objective Knowledge* (Oxford: Oxford University Press, 1972), chap. 3, pp. 119–22, and chap. 6, sections 14–17.

[3]Luigi Luca Cavalli-Sforza, *Genes, Peoples, and Languages* (Berkeley: University of California Press, 2000), p. 93, dates the origin of language at around 100,000 years ago, but given the above cited archeological evidence the later, more recent date of only 50,000 years ago appears more likely.

inter-subjectively reproducible and controllable. That is, by means of language knowledge could be transmitted to distant places and times (it was no longer tied to perception); one could communicate about matters (knowledge acquired and accumulated) far away in time and place. And because our reasoning process, our train of thought leading us to certain inferences and conclusions became 'objectified' in external, inter-subjectively ascertainable arguments it could not only be easily transferred through time and space but at the same time be publicly criticized, improved, and corrected. It is no wonder, then, that hand in hand with the emergence of language revolutionary changes in technology would come about.

About 100,000 years ago, the population size of "modern humans," our immediate predecessors, is estimated to have been around 50,000, spread across the African continent and northward into the Middle East, the region of today's Israel.[4] From about 80,000 to 70,000 years ago, the earth experienced a significant cooling period. As a consequence, the Neanderthals, who lived in Europe and in the course of many millennia had adjusted to cold climates moved southward, where they clashed with and apparently destroyed their African relatives in large numbers. In addition, an extended dry period beginning about 60,000 years ago robbed "modern man" of much of his subsistence basis, such that 50,000 years ago the number of "modern humans" may not have exceeded 5,000, confined to northeast Africa.[5]

---

[4]Ibid., p. 92.

[5]Wade, *Before the Dawn*, pp. 8, 58; Cavalli-Sforza's estimate is significantly higher: 50,000 (*Genes, Populations, and Language*, p. 50).

However, from then on the rise of modern humans has been uninterrupted, spreading all across the globe and eventually displacing all of their archaic relatives. The last Neanderthals, holed up in some caves near Gibraltar, are believed to have become extinct about 25,000 years ago. The last remnants of *homo erectus*, found on the Indonesian island of Flores, date back about 13,000 years.

The "modern humans" led a nomadic hunter-gatherer lifestyle. Societies were composed of small bands of people (10–30), which occasionally met and formed a common genetic pool of about 150 and may be up to 500 people (a size which geneticists have found to be necessary in order to avoid dysgenic effects[6]). The division of labor was limited, with the main partition being that between women — acting mostly as gatherers — and men — acting mostly as hunters. While private property of tools and implements was known and recognized, the nomadic lifestyle only allowed for little possessions and hence made hunter-gatherer societies comparatively egalitarian.[7] Nonetheless, life initially appears to

---

[6]Cavalli-Sforza, *Genes, Peoples, and Languages*, p. 30.

[7]The egalitarianism of hunter-gatherer societies should not be overemphasized or idealized, however. These societies were also characterized by pronounced hierarchical features. Not unlike what is known from the animal kingdom, men ranked above and dominated women. Often women were "taken" and treated by men like goods of the "outer" world are taken and treated: appropriated, stolen, used, abused, and traded. Children ranked below adults. Moreover, hierarchies existed among both male and the female members of society, down from the reigning alpha-male and female to the lowliest member of society. Status fights occurred, and whoever did not accept the established rank-order faced severe punishment. The losers in the fights for higher status were threatened with injury, even death and,

have been good for our forebears.[8] Only a few hours of regular work allowed for a comfortable life, with good (high protein) nourishment and plenty of leisure time. Indeed, fossil findings (skeletons and teeth) seem to indicate that our hunter-gatherer forebears enjoyed a life expectancy of well above 30 years, which was only reached again in the course of the nineteenth century.[9] Contra Hobbes, their life was anything but nasty, brutish, and short.[10]

However, the life of hunters and gatherers faced a fundamental and ultimately unanswerable challenge. Hunter-gatherer societies led essentially parasitic lives. That is, they did not add anything to the nature-given supply of goods. They only depleted the supply of goods. They did not produce (apart from a few tools) but only consumed. They did not grow and breed but had to wait for nature to regenerate and replenish. At best, what they accomplished was that they did not overhunt or overgather so that the natural regeneration process was not disturbed or even brought to an entire standstill. In any case, what this form of parasitism obviously

---

at the very best, expulsion from the tribe. In a word: even if tribal life provided for a comfortable standard of living in terms of abundant food and leisure it was anything but comfortable in terms of today's much cherished "individual autonomy." To the contrary, life in the tribal household meant discipline, order, and submission.

[8]See Richard Lee and I. De Vore, eds., *Man the Hunter* (Chicago: Aldine, 1968); Marvin Harris, *Cannibals and Kings: The Origins of Cultures* (New York: Vintage Books, 1977), esp. chap. 2.

[9]Harris, *Cannibals and Kings*, pp. 19f.

[10]This statement refers only to the hunter-gatherer life during periods of peace, however. On the high incidence of warfare and unnatural causes of death see pp. 27ff. below.

involved, then, was the inescapable problem of population growth. In order to permit the comfortable life just described, the population density had to remain extremely low. It has been estimated that one square mile of territory was needed to comfortably sustain one to two persons, and in less fertile regions even larger territories were necessary.[11] So what was one to do when the population size exceeded these more or less narrow limits?

People could of course try to prevent such population pressure from emerging, and indeed hunter-gatherer societies tried their best in this regard. They induced abortions, they engaged in infanticide, especially female infanticide, and they reduced the number of pregnancies by engaging in long periods of breast-feeding (which, in combination with the low body-fat characteristic of constantly mobile and moving women, reduces female fertility). Yet while this alleviated the problem it did not solve it. The population kept increasing.

Given that the population size could not be maintained at a stationary level, only three alternatives existed for the steadily emerging "excess" population. One could *fight* over the limited food supplies, one could *migrate*, or one could *invent* and adopt a new, technologically advanced societal organization-mode that allowed for a larger population size to survive on the same, given territory.

As for the first option, i.e., fighting, a few remarks shall suffice. In the literature, primitive man has been frequently described as peaceful and living in harmony with nature. Most

[11]Thus, for instance, writes Harris, *Cannibals and Kings*, p. 18: "In all of France during the late stone age there were probably no more than 20,000 and possibly as few as 1,600 human beings."

popular in this regard is Rousseau's portrayal of the "noble savage." Aggression and war, it has been frequently held, were the result of civilization built upon the institution of private property. In fact, matters are almost exactly the reverse.[12] True, the savagery of modern wars has produced unparalleled carnage. Both World War I and World War II, for instance, resulted in tens of millions of deaths and left entire countries in ruins. And yet, as anthropological evidence has in the meantime made abundantly clear, primitive man has been considerably more warlike than contemporary man. It has been estimated that on the average some 30 percent of all males in primitive, hunter-gatherer societies died from unnatural — violent — causes, far exceeding anything experienced in this regard in modern societies.[13] According to Lawrence Keeley's estimates, a tribal society on the average lost about 0.5 percent of its population in combat each year.[14] Applied to the population of the twentieth century this would amount to a casualty rate of some 2 billion people instead of the actual number of "merely" a few hundred million. Of course, primitive warfare was very different from modern warfare. It was not conducted by regular troops on battlefields, but by raids, ambushes, and surprise attacks. However, every attack was characterized by utmost brutality, carried out without mercy and always with deadly results; and while the number of people killed in each

---

[12]See Wade, *Before the Dawn*, chap. 8, and pp. 150–54; also Lawrence H. Keeley, *War Before Civilization* (New York: Oxford University Press, 1996).

[13]Napoleon Chagnon, "Life Histories, Blood Revenge, and Warfare in a Tribal Population," *Science* 239 (1988): 985–92.

[14]Keeley, *War Before Civilization*, p. 33; Wade, *Before the Dawn*, pp. 151f.

attack might have been small, the incessant nature of these aggressive encounters made violent death an ever-present danger for every man (and abduction and rape for every woman).[15] Moreover, increasing evidence for the widespread practice of cannibalism has been accumulated in recent times. Indeed, it appears that cannibalism was once upon a time an almost universal practice.[16]

More importantly, these findings regarding primitive man's warlikeness are not just anthropological curiosities, i.e., features that one might consider incidental to the true nature of hunter-gatherer societies. To the contrary, there exist fundamental theoretical reasons why such societies were characterized by incessant warfare and peaceful relations were almost impossible to attain, in particular if the possibility of evading one another was foreclosed because all surrounding land was

---

[15]See also Steven LeBlanc, *Constant Battles* (New York: St. Martin's Press, 2003).

[16]See Wade, *Before the* Dawn, pp. 154–58. Contrasting the ferocity of primitive vs. modern men, Wade, following Keeley, notes (*Before the Dawn*, p. 152):

> When primitive warriors met the troops of civilized societies in open battle, they regularly defeated them despite the vast disparity in weaponry. In the Indian wars, the U.S. Army "usually suffered severe defeats" when caught in the open, such as by the Seminoles in 1834, and at the battle of Little Bighorn. In 1879 the British army in South Africa, equipped with artillery and Gatling guns was convincingly defeated by Zulus armed mostly with spears and ox-hide shields at the battles of Isandlwana, Myer's Drift and Hlobane. The French were sent off by the Tuareg of the Sahara in the 1890s. The state armies prevailed in the end only through larger manpower and attritional campaigns, not by superior fighting skill.

occupied. Because then it became unavoidable that the members of different hunter-gatherer tribes encountered each other more or less regularly on their various expeditions in search of plants and animals. Indeed, as the population size increased such encounters became ever more frequent. And because hunters and gatherers did not add anything to the nature-given supply of goods but only consumed what was provided by nature, their competition for food was necessarily of an antagonistic nature: either I pick the berries or hunt a given animal or you do it. No or little trade and exchange between the members of different tribes existed, because the members of one tribe engaged in essentially the same activities as those of any other tribe and neither one accumulated any surplus of goods that could be exchanged for others' surplus-goods. There existed only ineradicable conflict and the more conflict the more the population number in each tribe exceeded its optimum size. In this situation, where everything appropriated by one person (or tribe) was immediately consumed and the total supply of goods was strictly limited by natural forces, only deadly antagonism could exist between men. In the words of Ludwig von Mises, men became "deadly foes of one another, irreconcilable rivals in their endeavors to secure a portion of the scarce supply of means of sustenance provided by nature. Each man would have been forced to view all other men as his enemies; his craving for the satisfaction of his own appetites would have brought him into an implacable conflict with all his neighbors. No sympathy could possibly develop under such a state of affairs."[17] Only the death of one's rivals provided a solution to one's own desire to survive. Indeed, to

[17]Ludwig von Mises, Mises, *Human Action: A Treatise on Economics* (Chicago: Regnery, 1966), p. 144.

spare another man's life would have left him equipped to create even more offspring and hence reduced one's own future chance of survival still further.[18]

The second available option to deal with the steadily re-emerging problem of excess population was migration. While by no means costless — after all one had to leave familiar for unfamiliar territories — migration (as compared to fighting)

[18]Indirectly, this insight into the irreconcilable antagonism between the members of different tribes within the framework of hunter-gatherer societies also provides a first clue as to the requirements for peaceful cooperation among men. In order for members of different tribes to view each other not as enemies but as potential collaborators, there must be genuine *production* of consumer goods (above and beyond the mere appropriation of nature-given consumer goods). At least, as a very minimum requirement, there must be production of consumer goods in the sense of the storage of surplus goods (of saving for future consumption). For only if man thus *adds* something to nature which otherwise, without his deliberate effort, would not exist at all, can there be a reason for one man to spare another man's life for his own good (for his own selfish motives and to his own advantage). To be sure, as proponents of the thesis that it is civilization, which breeds war, are fond to point out, the very fact that one man has added something to the supply of nature-given goods might also provide a reason for another man to engage in aggression: to rob him of his product. But there is certainly less reason to kill such a man than to kill a man who has added nothing but merely takes and consumes what is given (and hence inevitably reduces what remains available for another). Moreover, insofar as a man adds something to the total supply of available goods there exists also a reason for another man to *not* interfere with his activity but let him continue, and to benefit from him and his activity by engaging in mutually beneficial trade with him and hence, as a consequence, ultimately develop sympathetic feelings toward his fellow man. Thus, while civilization does not eliminate man's aggressive impulses it can and did diminish and attenuate them.

must have appeared frequently as the less costly option, especially as long as some open frontier existed. Hence, setting out from their homeland in East Africa, successively the entire globe was conquered by bands of people breaking away from their relatives to form new societies in areas hitherto unoccupied by humans.

It appears that this process began also about 50,000 years ago, shortly after the emergence of behaviorally modern man and the acquisition of the ability to build boats. From about this time on until around 12,000 to 11,000 years ago global temperatures gradually fell (since then we are in an interglacial warming period) and the sea levels accordingly fell.[19] People crossed over the Red Sea at the Gate of Grief, which was then merely a narrow gap of water dotted with islands, to land at the southern tip of the Arabian peninsula (which enjoyed a comparatively wet period at that time). From there onward,

[19]Actually, the last great warming period, also called interglacial period, had already ended about 120,000 years ago. During this period, i.e., more than 120,000 years ago, hippopotamuses had lived in the Rhine and the Thames and northern Europe had something of an "African appearance." From then on, glaciers moved steadily further southward and the sea level eventually fell by more than 100 meters. The Thames and the Elbe became tributaries of the Rhine, before it streamed first into the Northern Sea and from there into the Atlantic. See Josef H. Reichholf, *Eine kurze Naturgeschichte des letzten Jahrtausends* (Frankfurt/M.: Fischer, 2007), pp. 15f. When this period ended, quite suddenly, about 12,000 years ago, the glaciers rapidly retreated and the sea level rose, not by millimeters per year but very quickly in an almost flood-like fashion. Within a very brief period England and Ireland, which had previously been connected to the European continent, became islands. The Baltic Sea and much of the contemporary North Sea came thus into existence. Likewise, most of today's Persian Gulf dates from about this time. Ibid., pp. 49f.

preferring to stay in tropical climate zones to which one had been adjusted, the migration — of possibly not more than 150 people — continued eastward. Travel was mostly by boat, because until about 6,000 years ago when man learned how to tame horses, this form of transportation was much faster and more convenient than travel by foot. Hence, migration took place along the coastline — and proceeded from there into the interior through river valleys — first all the way to India. From there, as the genetic evidence seems to indicate, the population movement split into two directions. On the one hand it proceeded around the Indian peninsula to southeast Asia and Indonesia (which was then connected to the Asian mainland) and finally to the now foundered former continent of Sahul (of Australia, New Guinea, and Tasmania, which were joined until about 8,000 years ago), which was then only separated from the Asian mainland by a sixty mile wide channel of water dotted with islands permitting short-distance island hopping, as well as northward up the coast to China and eventually Japan. On the other hand, the migration process went from India in a northwesterly direction, through Afghanistan, Iran, and Turkey and ultimately Europe. As well, splitting off of this stream of migration, people pressed in a northeasterly direction into southern Siberia. Later migrations, most likely in three waves, with the first about 14,000–12,000 years ago, went from Siberia across the Bering Strait — then (until about 11,000 years ago) a land bridge — and onto the American continent, apparently reaching Patagonia only about 1,000 years later (archeological findings of human remains in southern Chile have been dated as 12,500 years old). The last migration route set out from Taiwan, which was occupied about 5,000 years ago, sailing across the Pacific to reach the Polynesian islands and finally, only about 800 years ago, New Zealand.[20]

The process was essentially always the same: a group invaded some territory, population pressure mounted, some people stayed put, a subgroup moved further on, generation after generation, along the coastline, following rivers and game and avoiding deserts and high mountains. The migration from Africa all the way to Australia may have taken about 4,000 to 5,000 years, and migration to Europe 7,000 years (the oldest artifacts there ascribed to modern humans, found in Bulgaria, date about 43,000 years back) and another 7,000 years to reach western Spain.[21] Once broken up, practically no contact existed between the various hunter-gatherer societies. Consequently, although initially closely related to one another through direct kinship relations, these societies formed separated genetic pools and, confronted with different natural environments and as the result of mutations and genetic drift interacting with natural selection, in the course of time they took on distinctly different appearances. By and large, the genetic difference between various societies increased in correlation with the spatial distance between societies and the duration of their separation time.[22] Different ethnicities emerged, and later also distinctly different human races. These emerging, genetically based differences concerned matters such as skin color, physical build

---

[20]For further details see Wade, *Before the Dawn,* chap. 5; also Jared Diamond, *Guns, Germs, and Steel: The Fates of Human Societies* (New York: Norton, 1997), chap. 1.

[21]See Cavalli-Sforza, *Genes, Populations, and Languages*, p. 94.

[22]Ibid., pp. 20–25.

and strength, resistance to cold temperatures and to various diseases, and tolerance *vis-à-vis* certain substances. They also concerned cognitive matters, however. Thus, genetic evidence exists for two significant further developments regarding the size and cognitive powers of the human brain. One such development occurred about 37,000 years ago and affected most of the population in Europe as well as in East Asia (but left very few traces in Africa), and another occurred about 6,000 years ago and affected mostly people in the Middle East and Europe (but had less impact in East Asia and almost none in sub-Saharan Africa).[23]

Moreover, hand in hand with the geographical and correlated genetic differentiation of humans went a linguistic differentiation. Very much in agreement with and supported by genetic (biological) evidence, some linguists, in particular Merritt Ruhlen,[24] following in the footsteps of the pioneering work of Joseph Greenberg, have made the plausible case for a single human proto-language, from which all human languages can be derived as more or less distant relatives. Obviously, the original emigrants from the African homeland, some 50,000 years ago, would have spoken the same language, and so it seems hardly surprising that the above-sketched population movement, and the splitting of groups of people into different genetic pools, more or less separated in time and space from one another, should be closely mirrored by a differentiation of languages, the grouping of different languages into language families, and the grouping of

---

[23] See Wade, *Before the Dawn*, pp. 96–99.

[24] Merritt Ruhlen, *The Origin of Language: Tracing the Evolution of the Mother Tongue* (New York: Wiley, 1994).

these into still larger super-families.[25] Likewise, the process of the proliferation of languages appears to have followed a predictable pattern. First, with the spread of humans around the world as hunters and gatherers and the concomitant proliferation of distinct, separated genetic pools, a successively increasing number of different languages emerged. Thus, for instance, of the 6,000 different languages still spoken today, some 1,200 languages are spoken in New Guinea, one of the most "primitive" remaining world regions, half of which have no more than the "magic" number of 500 speakers and none more than 100,000. Then, however, with the beginning of human settlement some 11,000 years ago and the following transition to agriculture and the attendant expansion and intensification of the division of labor (more on which later on), a countervailing and even contrary tendency appears to have come into existence: just as the genetic pools appear to have widened, so the number of different languages spoken has successively diminished.

II. THE PROBLEM: THEORY

About 35,000 years ago, i.e., 15,000 years after the initial exodus from Africa, practically all of Europe, Asia, Australia and, of course, Africa itself had been occupied by our ancestors, the modern humans, and archaic humans: *homo neanderthalensis* and *homo erectus*, were on the verge of extinction. About

[25]See Cavalli-Sforza, *Genes, Peoples, and Languages*, chap. 5, esp. p. 144 for a table showing the correlation between genetic and linguistic families and trees of descent. See also Luigi Luca Cavalli-Sforza and Francesco Cavalli-Sforza, *The Great Human Diasporas: The History of Diversity and Evolution* (Cambridge: Perseus Books, 1995), chap. 7; Wade, *Before the Dawn*, chap. 10, pp. 102ff.

12,000 years ago, humans had also spread all across the Americas. Apart from the Polynesian islands, then, all land and all of the naturally given supply of earthly (economic) goods: of plants and animals had been taken into human possession; and, given the parasitic lifestyle of hunter-gatherers, humans did not *add* anything to this land and the nature-given supply of goods but merely reacted to natural *changes*.

These changes were at times quite drastic. Changes in global climate, for instance, could and did significantly affect how much inhabitable land was available and the natural vegetation and animal population. In the time period under consideration, in the 20,000 plus years between 35,000 and 11,000 years ago, drastic changes in such natural conditions occurred. 20,000 years ago, for instance, during the period known as the *Last Glacial Maximum*, temperatures fell sharply and most of Northern Europe and Siberia became uninhabitable. Britain and all of Scandinavia was covered by glaciers, most of Siberia turned into polar desert and steppe-tundra extended as far south as the Mediterranean, the Black Sea, and the Caspian Sea. After 5,000 years, about 15,000 years ago, the glaciers began to retreat, allowing people, animals, and plants to re-occupy previously deserted regions. Twenty-five hundred years later, however, within merely a decade, temperatures again plummeted back to almost the previous frigid conditions; and only another 1,000 years later, about 11,500 years ago, and again quite suddenly, did temperatures then experience a long-sustained increase and the earth entered the so-called *Holocene*, the latest and still lasting interglacial warming period.[26] (The Sahara began to turn into the present,

[26]During the present *Holocene* period temperatures continued to show significant variations, however. About 10,000 years ago, after

extremely hot desert only less than 3,000 years ago. In pre-Roman times, the Sahara — and similarly the central Asian deserts — was still a green savanna with an abundant supply of wildlife. The power and the attraction of Carthage, for instance, was based largely on the fertility of its hinterland as a center of wheat production; this fact was an important reason for Rome's desire to destroy Carthage and gain control of its North African territories.[27])

In any case and regardless of all complicating details and all changes that future empirical researches will no doubt bring about concerning the foregoing historical narrative, at some point in time the landmass available to help satisfy human needs could no longer be enlarged. In economic jargon, the supply of the production factor "land" became fixed, and every increase in the size of the human population had to be sustained by the same, unchanged quantity of land. Of the formerly three available options in response to an increasing population pressure: to move, to fight, or to invent, only the latter two remained open. What to do when faced with this challenge?

---

a warming period of thousands of years, temperatures reached the present level. Several times thereafter, temperatures rose significantly above this level (by up to 2 degrees Celsius): 8,000 to 6,800 years ago, 6,000 to 5,500 years ago, 5,000 to 4,000 years ago, 2,500 to 2000 years ago, and again from the tenth to the fourteenth century, during the so-called medieval warming period. As well, several periods with significantly lower than present temperatures existed: 9,000 to 8,000 years ago, 6,800 to 6,000 years ago, 4,000 to 2,500 years ago, from the second to the eighth century and again from the fourteenth until the mid-nineteenth century, the so-called Little Ice Age. See Reichholf, *Eine kurze Naturgeschichte des letzten Jahrtausends*, p. 27.

[27]Ibid., pp. 23f.

To bring the problem faced into even sharper relief it is useful to first take another, more detailed look at the admittedly rather limited extent of the division of labor within a hunter-gatherer society.

So far the antagonism between the members of *different* bands or clans has been explained while it has been taken for granted that *within* a given band or clan collaboration — peaceful cooperation — exists. But why should this be so? Intra-group cooperation is almost universally assumed as a matter-of-course. Nonetheless, it too requires an explanation, because a world without even this limited degree of cooperation is certainly *conceivable*. To be sure, there exists a biological basis for *some* forms of human cooperation. "The mutual sexual attraction of male and female," writes Mises, "is inherent in man's animal nature and independent of any thinking and theorizing. It is permissible to call it original, vegetative, instinctive, or mysterious."[28] The same can be said about the relationship between mother and child. If mothers would not take care of their offspring for an extended period of time, their children would instantly die and mankind would be doomed. However, this necessary, biologically determined degree of cooperation is a far cry from that actually observed in hunter-gatherer societies. Thus, Mises continues,

> neither cohabitation, nor what precedes it or follows, generates social cooperation and societal modes of life. The animals too join together in mating, but they have not developed social relations. Family life is not merely a product of sexual intercourse. It is by no means natural and necessary that parents and children live together in the way they do in

[28]Ludwig von Mises, *Human Action*, p. 167.

> the family. The mating relation need not result in a family organization. The human family is an outcome of thinking, planning, and acting. It is this fact which distinguishes it radically from those animal groups which we call *per analogiam* animal families.[29]

Why, for instance, did not each man and each woman, after they had left infancy, hunt or gather alone only to meet for occasional sex? Why did it *not* occur what has been described as having occurred for *groups* of humans *already on the level of individuals*: one person, faced with a strictly limited supply of nature-given goods, breaking away from another in order to avoid conflict until all land was taken into possession and then a war of everyone against everyone else (rather than merely a war of the members of one group against the members of all other groups) breaking out? The answer to this is: because of the recognition that cooperation was more productive than isolated, self-sufficient action. Division of labor and cooperation based on such division of labor increased the productivity of human labor.

There are three reasons for this: First, there exist tasks which exceed the powers of any single man and require instead the combined efforts of several men in order to be successfully executed. Certain animals, for instance, might be too large or too dangerous to be hunted by single individuals but require the cooperative engagement of many. Or there exist tasks which could, in principle, be executed by a single individual but that would take up so much time for an isolated actor that the final result does not appear worth the effort. Only concerted action can accomplish these tasks in a time span sufficiently short in order to deem the task worthwhile. Searching for edible

[29]Ibid.

plants or animals, for instance, is fraught with uncertainties. On one day one might stumble across suitable plants or animals quickly, but at another time one might search for them in vain seemingly without end. But if one pools this risk, i.e., if a large number of gatherers or hunters begin their search separately only to call upon each other once anyone of them has turned out to be lucky in his search, then gathering and hunting might be turned into routinely successful endeavors for each participant.

Second: Even though the natural environment faced by each person might be more or less the same, each individual (even identical twins) is different from any other. Men, for instance, are significantly different in their abilities than women. By their very nature, men are typically better hunters and women better gatherers. Adults are significantly different in their abilities than kids. Some people are physically strong and others show great dexterity. Some are tall and others are quick. Some have great vision and others a good sense of smell. Given such differences it is obviously advantageous to partition the various tasks necessary to perform in order to secure a comfortable life in such a way that each person specializes in those activities in which he has an advantage over others. Women gather and men hunt. Tall individuals pick fruits from trees and short ones specialize in hunting mushrooms. Quick runners relay messages. Individuals with good eyesight will spot distant events. Kids are used for the exploration of small and narrow holes. People with great dexterity produce tools. The strong will specialize in going in for the kill, etc.

Third: Moreover, even if the members of one tribe are so distinguished from one another that one person is more efficient in every conceivable task than another, division of labor is still all-around more productive than isolated labor.

An adult might be better at any task than a kid, for instance. Given the inescapable fact of the scarcity of time, however, even in this conceivably worst-case scenario it makes economic sense — that is, it leads to a greater physical output of goods produced per unit of labor — if the adult specializes in those tasks in which his greater efficiency (as compared to that of the kid) is particularly pronounced and leaves those tasks for the kid to perform in which the latter's all-around lower efficiency is comparatively smaller. Even though the adult might be more efficient than the child in collecting small firewood, for instance, the adult's far greater superiority in hunting large game would make it a waste of his time to gather wood. Instead, he would want the child to collect fire wood and use all of his own precious time to perform that task in which his greater efficiency is especially marked, namely large game hunting.

Nonetheless: While these advantages offered by the division of labor can explain intratribal cooperation (rather than fight) and, based on such initially maybe purely "selfishly-motivated" collaboration, the gradual development of feelings of sympathy (good will) toward one's fellowmen, which go above and beyond whatever *biological* basis there may exist for the special, more-than-normally-friendly relationship between close kin, this explanation still only goes so far. Given the peculiar, parasitic nature of hunter-gatherer societies and assuming land to be fixed, invariably the moment must arise when the number of people exceeds the optimal group size and average living standards will fall, threatening whatever degree of intragroup solidarity previously might have existed.[30]

---

[30]Empirically, it appears that the "magic number," i.e., the optimum population size for a hunter-gatherer society, was somewhere between

This situation is captured and explained by the economic *law of returns.*

The law of returns, popularly but somewhat misleadingly also called the *law of diminishing returns*, states that for any combination of two or more production factors an optimum combination exists (such that any deviation from it involves material waste, or "efficiency losses").[31] Applied to the two original factors of production, labor and land (nature-given goods), the law implies that if one were to increase the quantity of labor (population) while the quantity of land and the available technology (hunting and gathering) remained fixed, eventually a point will be reached where the physical output per labor-unit input is maximized. This point marks the optimal population size. If there is no additional land available and technology remains fixed at a 'given' level, any population increase beyond the optimal size will lead to a progressive decline in per capita income. Living standards, on the

---

50 to 100 people for a territory of about 50 to 100 square miles (one person per square mile). At around this combination point, all advantages offered by the division of labor were exhausted. If the population size increased beyond this "magic" number, average living standards became increasingly endangered and this threat grew still more if neighboring tribes, due to their own internal population growth, increased their territorial incursions thus further diminishing the nature-given supply of goods available to the members of the first tribe. Internal as well as external population pressure then called for a solution to an increasingly urgent problem: namely sheer survival.

[31] See Mises, *Human Action*, pp. 127–131; idem, *Socialism: An Economic and Sociological Analysis* (Indianapolis: Liberty Classics, 1981), pp. 174–75; also Hans-Hermann Hoppe, *Kritik der sozialwissenschaftlichen Sozialforschung, Untersuchungen zur Grundlegung von Soziologie und Oekonomie* (Opladen: Westdeutscher Verlag, 1985), pp. 59–64.

average, will fall. A point of (absolute) overpopulation has been reached. This is, as Mises has termed it, the *Malthusian law of population.*

Because of the fundamental importance of this *Malthusian law of population* and in order to avoid any possible misunderstanding, it is advisable to make also explicit what the law does *not* state. The law does not assert where exactly this optimal combination point lies — at so-and-so many people per square mile, for instance — but only *that* such a point exists. Otherwise, if every quantity of output could be produced by increasing only one factor (labor) while leaving the other (land) unchanged, the latter (land) would cease to be scarce — and hence an economic good — at all; one could increase without limit the return of any piece of land by simply increasing the input of labor applied to this piece without ever having to consider expanding the size of one's land). The law also does not state that *every* increase of one factor (labor) applied to a fixed quantity of another (land) must lead to a less than proportional increase of the output produced. In fact, as one approaches the optimum combination point an increase of labor applied to a given piece of land might lead to a more than proportional increase of output (increasing returns). One additional man, for instance, might make it possible that an animal species can be hunted that cannot be hunted at all without this one extra hunter. The law of returns merely states that this cannot occur without definite limits. Nor does the law assert that the optimum combination point cannot be shifted upward and outward. In fact, as will be explained in the following, owing to technological advances the optimum combination point can be so moved, allowing a larger population to enjoy a higher average living standard on the same quantity of land. What the law of returns does say is only that *given* a state of technological development (mode of production) and a corresponding degree of specialization, an optimum combination point exists beyond which an increase in the supply of labor must necessarily lead to a less than proportional increase of the output produced or no increase at all.

Indeed, for hunter-gatherer societies the difficulties of escaping the Malthusian trap of absolute overpopulation are even more severe than these qualifications regarding the law of returns might indicate. For while these qualifications might leave the impression that it is "only" a technological innovation that is needed to escape the trap, this is not the full truth. Not just any technological innovation will do. Because hunter-gatherer societies are, as explained, "parasitic" societies, which do not add anything to the supply of goods but merely appropriate and consume what nature provides, any productivity increase *within* the framework of this mode of production does not (or only insignificantly so) result in a greater output of goods produced (of plants gathered or animals hunted) but rather merely (or mostly) in a reduction of the time necessary to produce an essentially unchanged quantity of output. The invention of bow and arrow that appears to have been made some 20,000 years ago, for instance, will not so much lead to a greater quantity of available animal meat to consume, thus allowing a larger number of people to reach or exceed a given level of consumption, but rather only to the same number of people enjoying more leisure with an unchanged standard of living in terms of meat consumption (or else, if the population increases, the gain of more leisure time will have to be paid for by a reduction in meat consumption per capita). In fact, for hunter-gatherers the productivity gains achieved by technological advances such as the invention of bow and arrow may well turn out to be no blessing at all or only a very short-term blessing. Because the greater ease of hunting that is thus brought about, for instance, may lead to overhunting, increasing the supply of meat per capita in the short-run, but diminishing or possibly eliminating the meat supply in the long-run by reducing the natural rate of animal reproduction or hunting animals to extinction and thus magnifying the Malthusian problem, even without any increase in population size.[32]

III. THE SOLUTION: THEORY AND HISTORY

The technological invention, then, that solved (at least temporarily[33]) the problem of a steadily emerging and re-emerging

---

[32]In fact, overhunting and animal extinction played a fateful role especially in the Americas, which were only occupied after the invention of bow and arrow. While the Americas originally exhibited pretty much the same fauna as the Eurasian continent — after all, for thousands of years animals could move from one continent to another across the Beringian land bridge — by the time of the European rediscovery of America some 500 years ago all large domesticable mammals (except for the llama in South America) had been hunted to extinction. Likewise, it appears now that the entire mega-fauna that once inhabited Australia was hunted to extinction (except for the red kangaroo). It seems that this event occurred around 40,000 years ago, only a few thousand years after man had first arrived in Australia, and even without the help of bow and arrow, only with very primitive weapons and the help of fires used for the trapping of animals. See on this Diamond, *Guns, Germs, and Steel*, pp. 42ff.

[33]While the changes brought about by the "Neolithic Revolution" allowed for a significantly higher sustainable population size, the Malthusian problem was bound to eventually arise again, and the seemingly ultimate solution to the problem was only reached with the so-called "Industrial Revolution" that began in Europe at the end of the seventeenth century. See on this the following chapter "From the

"excess" of population and the attendant fall of average living standards was a revolutionary change in the entire mode of production. It involved the change from a parasitic lifestyle to a genuinely productive life. Instead of merely appropriating and consuming what nature had provided, consumer goods were now actively produced and nature was augmented and improved upon.

This revolutionary change in the human mode of production is generally referred to as the "Neolithic Revolution": the transition from food production by hunting and gathering to food production by the raising of plants and animals.[34] It began about 11,000 years ago in the Middle East, in the region typically referred to as the "Fertile Crescent." The same invention was made again, seemingly independently, less than 2,000 years later in central China, and again a few thousand years later (about 5,000 years ago) also in the Western hemisphere: in Mesoamerica, in South America, and in the eastern part of today's United States. From these centers of innovation the new technology then spread to conquer practically the entire earth.

The new technology represented a fundamental cognitive achievement and was reflected and expressed in two interrelated institutional innovations, which from then on until today have become the dominant feature of human life: the appropriation and employment of ground land as private

---

Malthusian Trap To the Industrial Revolution: Reflections on Social Evolution."

[34]See also Michael H. Hart, *Understanding Human History* (Augusta, Ga.: Washington Summit Publishers, 2007), pp. 139ff.

property, and the establishment of the family and the family household.

To understand these institutional innovations and the cognitive achievement underlying them one must first take a look at the treatment of the production factor "land" by hunter-gatherer societies.

It can be safely assumed that private property existed within the framework of a tribal household. Private property certainly existed with regard to things such as personal clothing, tools, implements, and ornaments. To the extent that such items were produced by particular, identifiable individuals or acquired by others from their original makers through either gift or exchange they were considered individual property. On the other hand, to the extent that goods were the results of some concerted or joint effort they were considered collective household goods. This applied most definitely to the means of sustenance: to the berries gathered and the game hunted as the result of some intratribal division of labor. Without doubt, then, collective property played a highly prominent role in hunter-gatherer societies, and it is because of this that the term "primitive communism" has been often employed to describe primitive, tribal economies: each individual contributed to the household income "according to his abilities," and each received from the collective income "according to his needs" (as determined by the existing hierarchies within the group) — not quite unlike the "communism" in "modern" households.

Yet what about the ground land on which all group activities took place? One may safely rule out that ground land was considered private property in hunter-gatherer societies. But was it collective property? This has been typically assumed to be the case, almost as a matter-of-course. However, the question is in fact more complicated, because a third alternative exists: that ground land was neither private nor collective property but instead constituted part of the *environment* or more specifically the *general conditions* of action or what has also been called "common property" or in short "the commons."[35]

In order to decide this question standard anthropological research is of little or no help. Instead, some elementary as well as fundamental economic theory, including a few precise definitions, is required. The external world in which man's actions take place can be divided into two categorically distinct parts. One the one hand, there are those things that are considered *means* — or *economic goods*; and on the other hand, there are those things that are considered *environment* — or also referred to sometimes, if somewhat misleadingly, as *free goods*. The requirements for an element of the external world to be classified as a means or an economic good have been first identified with all due precision by Carl Menger.[36] They are threefold. First, in order for something to become an economic good (henceforth simply: a *good*), there must be a human need (an unachieved end or an unfulfilled human desire or want). Second, there must be the human perception of a thing believed to be equipped or endowed with properties or characteristics causally connected (standing in a causal connection) with, and hence capable of bringing about, the satisfaction of this need. Third, and most important in the present context, an element of the external world so perceived must be under human *control* such that it can be employed

[35]See on this distinction Murray N. Rothbard, *Man, Economy, and State* (Los Angeles: Nash, 1970), chap. 1.

[36]Carl Menger, *Principles of Economics* (Grove City, Pa.: Libertarian Press, [1871] 1994), p. 52.

(actively, deliberately used) to satisfy the given need (reach the end sought). Writes Mises: "A thing becomes a means when human reason plans to employ it for the attainment of some end and human action really employs it for this purpose."[37] Only if a thing is thus brought into a causal connection with a human need *and* this thing is under human control can one say that this entity is appropriated — has become a good — and hence, is someone's (private or collective) property. If, on the other hand, an element of the external world stands in a causal connection to a human need but no one can (or believes that he can) control and interfere with this element (but must leave it unchanged instead, left to its own natural devices and effects) then such an element must be considered part of the *un*appropriated environment and hence is no one's property. Thus, for instance, sunshine or rainfall, atmospheric pressure or gravitational forces may have a causal effect on certain wanted or unwanted ends, but insofar as man thinks himself incapable of interfering with such elements they are mere *conditions* of acting, not the part of any action. E.g., rainwater may be causally connected to the sprouting of some edible mushrooms and this causal connection may well be known. However, if nothing is done about the rainwater, then this water is also not owned by anyone; it might be a factor contributing to production, but it is not strictly speaking a production factor. Only if there is an actual interference with the natural rainfall, if the rainwater is collected in a bucket or in a cistern, for instance, can it be considered someone's property and does it become a factor of production.

Before the backdrop of these considerations one can now proceed to address the question regarding the status

[37]Mises, *Human Action*, p. 92.

of ground land in a hunter-gatherer society.[38] Certainly, the berries picked off a bush were property; but what about the bush, which was causally associated with the picked berries? The bush was only lifted from its original status as an environmental condition of action and a mere contributing factor to the satisfaction of human needs to the status of property and a genuine production factor once it had been appropriated: that is, once man had purposefully interfered with the natural causal process connecting bush and berries by, for instance, watering the bush or trimming its branches in order to produce a certain outcome (an increase of the berry harvest above the level otherwise, naturally attained). Further, once the bush had thus become property by grooming it or tending to it also *future* berry harvests became property, whereas previously only the berries actually harvested were someone's property; moreover, once the bush had been lifted out of its natural, unowned state by watering it so as to increase the future berry harvest, for instance, also the ground land supporting the bush had become property.

Similarly, there is also no question that a hunted animal was property; but what about the herd, the pack or the flock of which this animal was a part? Based on our previous considerations, the herd must be regarded as unowned nature as long as man had done *nothing* that could be interpreted (and that was in his own mind) causally connected with the satisfaction of a perceived need. The herd became property only once the requirement of *interfering* with the natural chain of events in order to produce some desired result had been

[38]See also Hans-Hermann Hoppe, *Eigentum, Anarchie und Staat. Studien zur Theorie des Kapitalismus* (Leipzig: Manuscriptum, [1987] 2005), chap. 4, esp. pp. 106ff.

fulfilled. This would have been the case, for instance, as soon as man engaged in the *herding* of animals, i.e., as soon as he actively tried to control the movements of the herd. The herder then did not only own the herd, he thus became also the owner of all future offspring naturally generated by the herd.

What, however, about the ground land on which the controlled movement of the herd took place? According to our definitions, the herdsmen could not be considered the owner of the ground land, at least not automatically so, without the fulfillment of a further requirement. Because herders as conventionally defined merely followed the natural movements of the herd and their interference with nature was restricted to keeping the flock together so as to gain easier access to any one of its members should the need for the supply of animal meat arise. Herdsmen did not interfere with the land itself, however. They did not interfere with the land in order to control the movements of the herd; they only interfered with the movements of the members of the herd. Land only became property once herders gave up herding and turned to animal husbandry instead, i.e., once they treated land as a (scarce) means in order to control the movement of animals by controlling land. This only occurred when land was somehow en-bordered, by fencing it in or constructing some other obstacles (such as trenches) which restricted the free, natural flow of animals. Rather than being merely a contributing factor in the production of animal herds, land thus became a genuine production factor.

What these considerations demonstrate is that it is erroneous to think of land as the collectively owned property of hunter-gatherer societies. Hunters were not herdsmen and still less were they engaged in animal husbandry; and gatherers were not gardeners or agriculturalists. They did not exercise control over the nature-given fauna and flora by tending to it or grooming it. They merely picked pieces from nature for the taking. Land to them was no more than a condition of their activities, not their property.

At best, very small sections of land had been appropriated (and were thus turned into collective property) by hunters and gatherers, to be used as permanent *storage* places for surplus goods for use at future points in time and as shelters, all the while the surrounding territories continued to be treated and used as unowned conditions of their existence.

What can be said, then, to have been the decisive step toward a (temporary) solution of the Malthusian trap faced by growing hunter-gatherer societies was the establishment of property in land going above and beyond the establishment of mere storage places and sheltering facilities. Pressured by falling standards of living as a result of absolute overpopulation, members of the tribe (separately or collectively) successively appropriated more and more of the previously unowned surrounding nature (land). And underlying and motivating this appropriation of surrounding ground land — and turning former places of storage and shelter into residential centers of agriculture and animal husbandry — was an eminent intellectual achievement. As Michael Hart has noted, "the idea of planting crops, protecting them, and eventually harvesting them is not obvious or trivial, and it requires a considerable degree of intelligence to conceive of that notion. No apes ever conceived of that idea, nor did *Australopithecus*, *Homo habilis*, *Homo erectus*, nor even archaic *Homo sapiens*."[39] Nor

---

[39]Hart, *Understanding Human History*, p. 162.

did any of them conceive of the even more difficult idea of the tending, taming, and breeding of animals.

Formerly, all consumer goods had been appropriated in the most direct and quickest way possible: through foraging, i.e., by "picking" such goods wherever they happened to be or go. In contrast, with agriculture and animal husbandry consumer goods were attained in an indirect and roundabout way: by producing them through the deliberate control of ground land. This was based on the discovery that consumer goods (plants and animals) were not simply 'given' to be picked, but that there were natural causes affecting their supply *and* that these natural causes could be manipulated by taking control of ground land. The new mode of production required more time in order to reach the ultimate goal of food consumption (and insofar involved a loss of leisure), but by interposing ground land as a genuine factor of production it was more productive and led to a greater total output of consumer goods (food), thus allowing for a larger population size to be sustained on the same quantity of land.[40]

More specifically with respect to plants: Seeds and fruits suitable for nutritional purposes were no longer just picked (and possibly stored), but the wild plants bearing them were actively cultivated. Besides for their taste, seeds and fruits were selected for size, durability (storability), the ease of harvesting and of seed-germination, and they were not consumed but used as inputs for the *future* output of consumer

[40]It has been estimated that with the appropriation of land and the corresponding change from a hunter-gatherer existence to that of agriculturists-gardeners and animal husbandry a population size ten to one hundred times larger than before could be sustained on the same amount of land.

goods, leading in the relatively short time span of maybe twenty to thirty years to new, domesticated plant varieties with significantly improved yields per unit land. Among the first plants thus domesticated in the Near and Middle East were the einkorn wheat, emmer wheat, barley, rye, peas, and olives. In China it was rice and millet; much later, in Mesoamerica it was corn, beans, and squash; in South America potatoes and manioc; in Northeast America sunflowers and goosefoot; and in Africa sorghum, rice, yams, and oil palm.[41]

The process of animal domestication proceeded along similar lines, and in this regard it was possible to draw on the experience gained by the first domestication and breeding of dogs, which had taken place some 16,000 years ago, i.e., still under hunter-gatherer conditions, somewhere in Siberia.[42]

Dogs are the descendants of wolves. Wolves are excellent hunters. However, they are also scavengers, and it has been plausibly argued that as such wolves regularly hung around human campsites for scraps. As scavengers, those wolves who were least afraid of humans and who displayed the friendliest behavior toward them obviously enjoyed an evolutionary advantage. It was likely from these semi-tame, camp-following wolves that cubs were adopted into tribal households as pets and where it was then discovered that these could be trained for various purposes. They could be used in the hunt of other animals, they could be used to pull, they made for good bed-warmers during cold nights, and they even provided a source of meat in cases of emergency. Most importantly, however, it was discovered that some of the dogs could bark

---

[41]Diamond, *Guns, Germs, and Steel*, pp. 100, 167.

[42]Wade, *Before the Dawn*, pp. 109–13.

(wolves rarely bark) and be selected and bred for their ability to bark and as such perform the invaluable task of warning and guarding their owners of strangers and intruders. It was this service above all, that appears to be the reason why, once the dog had been "invented," this invention spread like wildfire from Siberia all across the world. Everyone everywhere wanted to possess some offspring of this new, remarkable kind of animal, because in an era of constant intertribal warfare, the ownership of dogs proved to be a great advantage.[43]

Once the dog had arrived in the region of the Near East, which was to become the first center of human civilization, it must have added considerable momentum to the human "experiment" of productive living and its success. For while a dog used for sentry duty was an asset for mobile hunter-gatherers, it was an even greater asset for stationary settlers. The reason for this is straightforward: because in sedentary societies there were simply *more* things to be protected. In hunter-gatherer societies one had to fear for one's life, be it from external or internal aggression. However, because no member of society owned much of anything, there was little or no reason to steal. Matters were different, though, in a society of settlers. From its very inception, sedentary life was marked by the emergence of significant differences in the property and wealth owned by different members of society; hence, insofar as envy existed in any way, shape, or form (as can

[43]Incidentally, genetic analyses have revealed that all present dogs, including those in the Americas, stem most likely from a single litter to be located somewhere in East Asia. That is, it appears that the domestication of the dog did not occur independently at various places but at a single place from where it spread outward to ultimately encompass the entire globe.

be safely assumed)[44] each member (each separate household) also faced the threat of theft or destruction of his property by others, including especially also members of his own tribe. Dogs provided invaluable help in dealing with this problem, especially because dogs, as a matter of biological fact, attach themselves to *individual "masters,"* rather than to people in general or, like cats, for instance, to particular places.[45] As such, they themselves represented a prime example of something owned *privately*, rather than collectively. That is, they offered a "natural refutation" of whatever taboo might have existed in a primitive society against the private ownership of property. Moreover and more importantly, because dogs were unquestionably the property of particular individuals they proved also uniquely serviceable in guarding the private property of their natural owners from every kind of "foreign" invader.[46]

Animals, even more so than plants, were valuable for humans for a variety of reasons: as sources of meat, milk, skin, fur, and wool and also as potential means of transportation, pull, and traction, for instance. However, as a matter of biological fact, most animals turn out to be *un*domesticable.[47] The first and foremost selection criterion, then, in the

---

[44]See Helmut Schoeck, *Envy: A Theory of Social Behavior* (New York: Harcourt, Brace & World, 1970).

[45]See Konrad Lorenz, *Man Meets Dog* (New York: Routledge, 2002; original German edition 1954).

[46]Remarkably, even today, with the availability of highly sophisticated electronic alarm systems, it remains barking dogs which offer the most effective protection against burglary.

[47]See Diamond, *Guns, Germs, and Steel*, chap. 9, esp. pp. 168–75.

"production" of animals as livestock or pets was an animal species' perceived degree of tame-ability or controllability. To test one's hypothesis, in a first step it was checked whether or not an animal was suitable to herding. If so, it was then tried if a herd of wild animals could also be penned. If so, one would subsequently select the tamer animals as parents of the next generation — but not all animals breed in captivity! — and so on and on. Finally, one would select among the tamed animal variety for other desirable properties such as size, strength, etc., thus breeding eventually a new, domesticated animal species. Among the first large mammalian animals thus domesticated in the Near and Middle East (around 10,000 years ago) were sheep, goats, and pigs (from wild boars), then cattle (from wild aurochs). Cattle were also domesticated, apparently independently, in India at about the same time (about 8,000 years ago). Roughly at about the same time as in the Near and Middle East, sheep, goats, and pigs were domesticated independently also in China, and China was also to contribute the domesticated water buffalo (about 6,000 years ago). Central Asia and Arabia contributed the domesticated Bactrian and Arabian camel respectively (around 4,500 years ago). And the Americas, or more precisely the Andes region of South America, were to contribute the guinea pig (about 7,000 years ago), the llama and alpaca (about 5,500 years ago). Finally, an "invention" of particularly momentous consequences was the domestication of the horse, which occurred about 6,000 years ago in the region of today's Russia and Ukraine. This achievement initiated a genuine revolution in land transportation. Up until then, on land man had to walk from place to place, and the fastest way to cover distances was by boat. This changed dramatically with the arrival of the domesticated horse, which from then on until the nineteenth century with the invention of the locomotive and the motorcar, was to provide the fastest means of overland transportation. Accordingly, not quite unlike the "invention" of the dog some 16,000 years ago, the "invention" of the horse was to spread like wildfire. However, coming some 10,000 years later, the latter invention could no longer diffuse as widely as the former. While the dog had reached practically all corners of the world, the climatic changes — the global warming — that had taken place in the meantime made it impossible for the same success to be repeated in the case of the horse. In the meantime, the Eurasian land mass was separated from the Americas and from Indonesia, New Guinea, and Australia by bodies of water too wide to be bridged. Thus, it was only thousands of years later, after the European *re*discovery of the Americas, for instance, that the horse was finally introduced there. (Wild horses had apparently existed on the American continent, but they had been hunted to extinction there so as to make any independent domestication impossible.)

The appropriation of land as property and basis of agriculture and animal husbandry was only half of the solution to the problem posed by an increasing population pressure, however. Through the appropriation of land a more effective use was made of land, allowing for a larger population size to be sustained. But the institution of land ownership in and of itself did not affect the other side of the problem: the continued proliferation of new and more offspring. This aspect of the problem required some solution as well. A social institution had to be invented that brought this proliferation under control. The institution designed to accomplish this task is the institution of the family, which developed not coincidentally hand in hand with that of land ownership.

Indeed, as Malthus pointed out, in order to solve the problem of overpopulation, along with the institution of private property "the commerce between the sexes" had to undergo some fundamental change as well.[48]

What was the commerce between the sexes before and what was the institutional innovation brought about in this regard by the family? A precise answer to the first question is notoriously difficult, but it is possible to identify the principal structural change. In terms of economic theory, the change can be described as one from a situation where both the benefits of creating offspring — by creating an additional potential *producer* — and especially the costs of creating offspring — by creating an additional *consumer* (eater) — were socialized. That is, reaped and paid for by society at large rather than the "producers" of this offspring, to a situation where both benefits as well as costs involved in procreation were internalized by and economically imputed back to those individuals causally responsible for producing them.

Whatever the details may have been, it appears that the institution of a stable monogamous and also of a polygamous relationship between men and women that is nowadays associated with the term family is fairly new in the history of mankind and was preceded for a long time by an institution that may be broadly defined as "unrestricted" or "unregulated" sexual intercourse or as "group marriage."[49] The commerce between the sexes during this stage of human history

---

[48]*Essay on the Principle of Population*, chap. 10.

[49]See on this Friedrich Engels, *Der Ursprung der Familie, des Privateigentums und des Staates*, in: Marx/Engels, *Werke*, Band 21 (Berling: Dietz Verlag, [1884] 1972).

did not rule out the existence of temporary pair relationships between one man and one woman. However, in principle every woman was considered a potential sexual partner of every man, and vice versa. "Männer (lebten) in Vielweiberei und ihre Weiber gleichzeitig in Vielmännerei," noted Friedrich Engels, following in the footsteps of Lewis H. Morgan's researches in *Ancient Society* (1871), "und die gemeinsamen Kinder (galten) daher auch als ihnen allen gemeinsam (gehörig). …. jede Frau (gehörte) jedem Mann und jeder Mann jeder Frau gleichmässig."[50]

---

[50]Ibid., pp. 38f. "Men lived in polygamy and their women simultaneously in polyandry, and their children were considered as belonging to all of them. …. Each woman belonged to every man and each man to every woman."

Incidentally, socialist authors such as Friedrich Engels did not merely describe but glorify this institution, very much like they glorified the already mentioned institution of "primitive communism." Indeed, socialists typically recognized, quite correctly, the joint emergence of private property and the institution of the family, and they thought (and hoped) that both institutions — private property in the means of production, including land, and the (monogamous) family — would ultimately disappear again with the establishment of a future socialist society characterized by plenty (plentitude) of wealth and free love. Thus, after an arduous if necessary historical detour characterized by misery, exploitation, and male sexual domination, mankind would at long last return — on a higher level — to the very institutions characteristic of its own prehistoric "golden age." Under socialism, monogamous marriage was to disappear along with private property. Choice in love would become free again. Men and women would unite and separate as they pleased. And in all of this, as socialist August Bebel wrote in his (at the times in the 1880s and 1890s) enormously popular book *Die Frau und der Sozialismus*, socialism would not create anything really new, but only "recreate on a higher level of culture and under new social forms what was universally valid on a more primitive

What Engels and countless later socialists failed to notice in their glorifying description of the past — and supposedly again future — institution of "free love," however, is the plain fact that this institution has a direct and clear effect on the production of offspring. As Ludwig von Mises has commented: "it is certain that even if a socialist community may bring 'free love,' it can in no way bring free birth."[51] What Mises implied with this remark, and what socialists such as Engels and Bebel apparently ignored, is that, certainly in the age before the availability of effective means of contraception, free love has consequences, namely pregnancies and births, and that births involve benefits as well as costs. This does not matter as long as the benefits exceed the costs, i.e., as long as an additional member of society adds more to it as a producer of goods than it takes from it as a consumer — and this may well be the case for some time. But it follows from the law of returns that this situation cannot last forever, without limits. Inevitably, the point must arrive when the costs of additional offspring will exceed its benefits. Then, any further procreation must be stopped — moral restraint must be exercised — unless one wants to experience a progressive fall in average living standards. However, if children are considered everyone's or no one's children, because everyone entertains sexual relations with everyone else, then the incentive to refrain from procreation disappears or is at least significantly diminished. Instinctively, by virtue of man's biological nature, each

---

cultural level and before private ownership dominated society." Bebel, *Die Frau und der Sozialismus*, 1st ed. (Stuttgart, 1879), p. 343; 62nd ed. East-Berlin, 1973: www.mlwerke.de/beb/beaa/beaa_000.htm; see also Ludwig von Mises, *Socialism*, p. 87.

[51]Ludwig von Mises, *Socialism*, p. 175.

woman and each man is driven to spread and proliferate her or his genes into the next generation of the species. The more offspring one creates the better, because the more of one's genes will survive. No doubt, this natural human instinct can be controlled by rational deliberation. But if no or little economic sacrifice must be made for simply following one's animal instincts, because all children are maintained by society at large, then no or little incentive exists to employ reason in sexual matters, i.e., to exercise any moral restraint.

From a purely economic point of view, then, the solution to the problem of overpopulation should be immediately apparent. The ownership of children or more correctly the trusteeship over children must be privatized. Rather than considering children as collectively owned by or entrusted to "society" or viewing childbirths as some uncontrolled and uncontrollable natural event and accordingly considering children as owned by or entrusted to no one (as mere favorable or unfavorable "environmental changes"), children must instead be regarded as entities which are privately produced and entrusted into private care. As Thomas Malthus first perceptively noted, this, essentially, is what is accomplished with the institution of a family:

> the most natural and obvious check (on population) seemed to be to make every man provide for his own children; that this would operate in some respect as a measure and guide in the increase of population, as it might be expected that no man would bring beings into the world, for whom he could not find the means of support; that where this notwithstanding was the case, it seemed necessary, for the example of others, that the disgrace and inconvenience attending such a conduct should fall upon the individual, who had thus inconsiderately plunged himself and innocent children in misery and want. — The institution of marriage, or at

> least, of some express or implied obligation on every man to support his own children, seems to be the natural result of these reasonings in a community under the difficulties that we have supposed.[52]

Moreover and finally: with the formation of monogamous or polygamous families came another decisive innovation. Earlier on, the members of a tribe formed a single, unified household, and the intratribal division of labor was essentially an intra-household division of labor. With the formation of families came the breakup of a unified household into several, independent households and with that also the formation of "several" — or private — ownership of land. That is, the previously described appropriation of land was not simply a transition from a situation where something that was earlier on unowned became now owned, but more precisely something previously unowned was turned into something owned by separate households (thus allowing also for the emergence of interhousehold division of labor).

Consequently, then, the higher social income made possible by the ownership of land was no longer distributed as was formerly the case: to each member of society "according to his need." Rather, each separate household's share in the total social income came to depend on the product economically imputed to it, that is, to its labor and its property invested in production. In other words: the formerly pervasive "communism" might have still continued *within* each household, but communism vanished from the relation between the members of different households. The incomes of different households differed, depending on the quantity and quality of invested labor and property, and no one had a claim on

[52]*Essay on the Principle of Population*, chap. 10.

the income produced by the members of a household other than one's own. Thus, "free riding" on others' efforts became largely if not entirely impossible. He who did not work could no longer expect to still eat.[53]

---

[53]Rationally motivated as the institution of the family was, the transition from a regime of "free love" to one of family life did not come without costs, and the associated benefits and costs were different for men and women.

Surely, from the male's point of view it was advantageous to have every woman accessible for sexual gratification. In addition, this greatly improved his chances of reproductive success. By having children with as many women as possible the likelihood of his genes being passed on into future generations was increased. And this was accomplished seemingly without any cost to him if the responsibility of raising children to maturity could be externalized onto society at large. In contrast, if sexual access was restricted to just one woman (in the case of monogamy) or a few women (in the case of polygamy) his chances of sexual gratification and of reproductive success were diminished. Moreover, men now had to weigh and compare the pros (benefits) and cons (costs) of sex and procreation — something they previously did not have to do. On the other hand, also primitive men could not fail to notice, at least eventually, that even under a regime of free love the chances of sexual gratification and reproductive success were by no means equal. Some males — the stronger and more attractive alpha males — had much better chances than others. In fact, as every animal breeder knows, just one male is sufficient to keep all females constantly impregnated. Thus, free love effectively meant that very few males "had" most of the women, and especially most of the attractive and reproductively most appealing women, and fathered most of the offspring, while most of the males had the dubious obligation of helping to bring up other men's children. Surely, even the dimmest recognition of this fact must have posed a permanent threat to any intratribal solidarity and especially to any inter-male solidarity that was called for, for instance, in the defense against rival tribes; and this threat must have grown ever more intense the farther the population exceeded its optimum size. In contrast, the institution of a monogamous family and to a somewhat lesser degree also of a polygamous family offered to each male a somewhat equal chance of reproductive success and thus created a much greater incentive for every male to engage and invest in cooperative behavior.

Matters are significantly different from the female point of view. After all, it is women who must bear the risk of pregnancy associated with sexual intercourse. It is they who are particularly vulnerable during pregnancy and following childbirth. Moreover, it is women who have a unique natural tie to children; for while there can be always some doubt as to paternity no doubt is possible as far as maternity is concerned. Every woman knows who *her* children are and who the children of *other* women are. In light of these natural facts the principal advantage of a regime of free love from a female point of view becomes apparent. Because of the greater risk and investment associated with sex for women, women tend to be more selective as far as their mating partner is concerned. Thus, in order to increase the likelihood of their own reproductive success, they exhibit a strong preference for mating partners who appear healthy, vigorous, attractive, bright, etc., i.e., in a word: for alpha males. And because males are less choosy in their selection of sex objects, under a system of free love even the least attractive females can realistically expect to be able to mate occasionally with some of the most attractive males and hence possibly pass their "superior" genes on to one's own offspring. Obviously, this advantage disappears as soon as the institution of the family replaces a regime of free love. Each woman is now supposed to try her reproductive luck with just one or maybe a few sets of male genes, and in the great majority of cases these genes do not rank among the very best. What did women get out of marriage, then? Very little, it would seem, as long as the population was at or around its optimum size and the life of the hunter-gatherer tribe was characterized by comfort and plenty. This had to change, however, as soon as the population grew beyond this point. The more the population exceeded its optimum size the more intense grew the competition for the limited food supplies. Whatever inter-female solidarity existed before increasingly weakened now. Naturally, each woman was interested in assuring her own reproductive success and helping her own children reach maturity and thus came into conflict with every other woman and her children. Even killing another woman's child in order to further the prospect of survival for one's own children was increasingly considered an option in this situation. (Incidentally, the same sort of inter-female competition for reproductive success still prevails to some extent within the framework of polygamous relationships and explains some of the peculiar instabilities and tensions inherent in such relationships.) In this situation, each woman (and her kids) is in increasing need for personal protection. But who would be willing to provide such protection? Most children have the same father — from among the few alpha males endowed with more-than-equal chances of procreation — but they have different mothers. Accordingly, the protection of one woman and her children from another cannot be expected to come from the children's father, because the father is very often the same one. Nor can it be expected to come from another male; for why should a male offer personal support and protection to a woman who entertained sexual relations with other men and whose children were fathered by other men, especially if this offspring threatened his own standard of living? A woman could only secure personal protection from a man if she forewent all of the advantages of free love and promised instead to grant her sexual favors exclusively to him and thus managed to assure him also that her children were always his as well.

Distinctly male and female perspectives exist not only as far as the very establishment of the institution of the family is concerned but also regarding the importance of marital fidelity in maintaining its stability. The difference between male and female calculations in this regard has its reason in the natural fact that, at least until the very recent development of reliable genetic paternity tests, a child's mother was always known in a way — with a degree of certainty — that was unavailable and unattainable for the child's father. As folk wisdom has it: mother's baby, father's maybe. This fact, again quite "naturally," had to lead to significantly different — asymmetric — expectations regarding appropriate (and inappropriate) male and female marital conduct. Of course, in order to assure the stability of the institution of

Thus, in response to mounting population pressure a new mode of societal organization had come into existence, displacing the hunter-gatherer lifestyle that had been characteristic of most of human history. As Ludwig von Mises summarized the matter:

---

the family any form of marital infidelity had to be socially disapproved; but disapproval had to be far more pronounced and the possible sanctions far more severe in the case of female infidelity than in the case of male infidelity. While this may appear "unfair," it was in fact quite rational and in accordance with the "nature of things," because female infidelity involved a far greater risk for betrayed husbands than male infidelity involved for betrayed wives. A wife's infidelity can be the first step leading to a divorce from her husband just as a husband's infidelity can be the first step leading to a divorce from his wife. In this regard, the situation is the same (symmetric) in both cases and the "sin" committed is equally grave. However, if and insofar as marital infidelity does *not* lead to divorce, the "sin" committed by a woman must be considered far graver than that committed by a man. Because extramarital sexual affairs may lead to pregnancies, and if a so-impregnated woman then stays with her husband, the real danger arises that she might be tempted to present her illegitimate offspring to her husband as his own, thus deceiving him to support another man's child. No such danger exists in the opposite case: no man can submit his illegitimate offspring to his wife without her knowing the truth of the matter. Hence, the far greater social stigma attached to female as compared to male infidelity. (Incidentally — and also quite rationally — in the case of male infidelity a similar distinction is made: the offense is considered more severe if a man has an affair with a married woman than with an unmarried one; for in the former case he becomes a potential accomplice to a further female act of deception whereas in the latter case he does not. Accordingly, in recognition of this distinction and so as to accommodate the rather indiscriminate male sex drive, prostitution has become a near-universal social institution.)

> Private ownership in the means of production is the regulating principle which, within society, balances the limited means of subsistence at society's disposal with the less limited ability of consumers to increase. By making the share in the social product which falls to each member of society depend on the product economically imputed to him, that is, to his labour and his property, the elimination of surplus human beings by the struggle for existence, as it rages in the vegetable and animal kingdom, is replaced by a reduction in the birth-rate as a result of social forces. "Moral restraint," the limitations of offspring imposed by social positions, replaces the struggle for existence.[54]

Having first established some permanent storage and sheltering places, then, step by step, having appropriated more and more surrounding land as the basis for agricultural production and the raising of livestock and transforming erstwhile centers of storage and shelter into extended settlements composed of houses and villages occupied by separate family households, the new lifestyle of the people of the Near and Middle East as well as the other regions of original human settlement began to spread outward, slowly but inescapably.[55] In principle, two modes are conceivable by which this diffusion could have taken place. Either the original settlers gradually displaced the neighboring nomadic tribes in search of new to-be-cultivated land (demic diffusion), or else the latter imitated and adopted the new lifestyle on their own initiative (cultural diffusion). Until recently, it had been generally

---

[54]Mises, *Socialism*, p. 282.

[55]Based on archeological records, the speed of this diffusion process has been estimated at about one kilometer per year on land (and somewhat higher along coastlines and river valleys). See Cavalli-Sforza, *Genes, Peoples, and Languages*, p. 102.

believed that the first mode of diffusion was the predominant one.[56] However, based on newly discovered genetic evidence this view now appears to be questionable, at least insofar as the spread of the new, sedentary lifestyle from the Near East to Europe is concerned. If present Europeans were the descendants of Near Eastern people at the time of the Neolithic Revolution, genetic traces for this should exist. In fact, however, very few such traces can be found among present-day Europeans. Thus, it appears more likely that the spread of the new sedentary lifestyle occurred largely, if not exclusively, via the latter, second-mentioned route, while the role in this process played by the original Near Eastern settlers was only a minor one. Perhaps a few such settlers pushed in a northern and western direction, where they were then absorbed by neighboring people adopting their new and successful lifestyle, with the effect that their own genetic imprint became more and more diluted with increasing distance from their Near Eastern point of origin.

In any case, with the Neolithic Revolution the formerly universal hunter-gatherer lifestyle essentially died out or was relegated to the outer fringes of human habitation. Without doubt, the newly developing farming communities were attractive targets for nomadic raiders, and owing to their greater mobility neighboring nomadic tribes for a long time posed a serious threat to agricultural settlers. But ultimately, nomads were no match for them, because of their greater numbers. More specifically, it was the organization of larger numbers of people in communities of households — the

[56]See for instance Cavalli-Sforza, *Genes, Peoples, and Languages*, pp. 101–13; Cavalli-Sforza & Cavalli-Sforza, *The Great Human Diasporas*, chap. 6, esp. pp. 144ff.

location of separate households in close physical proximity to each other — that made for military superiority. Community life did not merely lower the transaction costs as far as intratribal exchange was concerned. Community life also offered the advantage of easily and quickly coordinated joint defense in the case of external aggression. Moreover, besides the strength of greater numbers, settled agricultural communities allowed also for an intensified and expanded division of labor and for greater savings and thus facilitated the development of a weaponry superior to anything available to bands of nomads.[57]

Fifty thousand years ago the human population size has been estimated to have been as low as 5,000 or possibly 50,000 people. At the beginning of the Neolithic Revolution, some 11,000 years ago, when essentially the entire globe had been conquered by tribes of hunters and gatherers having spread out in the course of thousands of years from their original homeland somewhere in East Africa, the world population size has been estimated to have reached about

---

[57]More than 10,000 years ago already some early-neolithic settlements, such as Catal Höyük in present-day Turkey, for instance, reached an estimated size of 4,000–5,000 inhabitants. Findings made at such sites include sanctuaries à la Stonehenge (alas, more than 6,000 years older!), spacious houses built of stone and with elaborate wall paintings, megalith columns with animal-reliefs, sculptures, carvings with writing-like symbols, ornaments, stone-vessels with elaborate decorations, stone-daggers, mirrors made from obsidian (a volcanic stone), bone needles, arrow heads, millstones, jugs and vases made of stone and clay, rings and chains made from colorful stones, even the beginning of metal works.

four million.[58] Since then, slowly but steadily, the new mode of production: of agriculture and animal husbandry based on private (or collective) ownership of land and organized around separate family households, successively displaced the original hunter-gatherer order. Consequently, at the beginning of the Christian era, the world population had increased to 170 million, and in 1800, which marks the onset of the so-called Industrial Revolution (the topic of the following chapter) and the close of the agrarian age or as it also been termed the "old biological order," it had reached 720 million. (Today's world population exceeds seven billion!) During this agrarian age, the size of cities occasionally reached or even surpassed one million inhabitants, but until the very end less than 2 percent of the population lived in big cities and even in the economically most advanced countries 80–90 percent of the population was occupied in agricultural production (while this number has fallen to less than 5 percent today).

---

[58]See Colin McEvedy & Richard Jones, *Atlas of World Population History*, Harmondsworth: Penguin Books, 1978.

2

FROM THE MALTHUSIAN TRAP TO THE INDUSTRIAL REVOLUTION: REFLECTIONS ON SOCIAL EVOLUTION

I. ECONOMIC THEORY

For economic theory the question of how to increase wealth and get rich has a straightforward answer.

It has three components: you get richer (a) through capital accumulation, i.e., the construction of intermediate "producer" or "capital" goods that can produce more consumer goods per unit time than can be produced without them or goods that cannot be produced at all with just land and labor (and capital accumulation in turn has something to do with (low) time preference); (b) through participation and integration in the division of labor; and (c) through population control, i.e., by maintaining the optimal population size.

Robinson Crusoe, alone on his island, has originally only his own "labor" and "land" (nature) at his disposal. He is as rich (or poor) as nature happens to make him. Some of his most urgently felt needs he may be able to satisfy directly, equipped only with his bare hands. At the very least, he can always satisfy his desire of leisure in this way: immediately. However, the satisfaction of most of his wants requires more than bare nature and hands, i.e., some indirect or roundabout — and time-consuming — production method. Most, indeed almost all goods and associated sorts of satisfaction require the help of some only indirectly useful tools: of producer or capital goods. With the help of producer goods it becomes possible to produce more per unit time of the very goods that can be produced also with bare hands (such as leisure) or to produce goods that cannot be produced at all with just land and labor. In order to catch more fish than with his bare hands Crusoe builds a net; or in order to build a shelter that he cannot build with his bare hands at all, he must construct an axe.

However, to build a net or an axe requires a sacrifice (saving). To be sure, production with the help of producer goods is expected to be more productive than without it; Crusoe would not spend any time building a net if he did not expect that he could catch more fish per unit time with the net than without it. Nonetheless, the production of a producer good involves a sacrifice; for it takes time to build a producer good and the same time cannot be used for the enjoyment or consumption of leisure or other immediately available consumer goods. In deciding whether or not to build the productivity enhancing net, Crusoe must compare and rank two expected states of satisfaction: the satisfaction which he can attain now, without any further waiting, and the satisfaction that he can attain only later, after a longer waiting time. In deciding to build the net, Crusoe has determined that he ranks the sacrifice: the value forgone of greater consumption now, in the present, below the reward: the value of greater consumption later, in the future. Otherwise, if he had ranked these magnitudes differently, he would have abstained from building the net.

This weighing and the possible exchange of present against future goods and associated satisfactions are governed by time preference. Present goods are invariably more valuable than future ones, and we exchange the former against the latter only at a premium. The degree, however, to which present goods are preferred to future ones, or the willingness to forgo some possible present consumption for a greater future consumption, i.e., the willingness to save, is different from person to person and one point in time to another. Depending on the height of his personal time preferences Crusoe will save and invest more or less and his standard of living will be higher or lower. The lower his time preference, i.e., the easier it is for Crusoe to delay current gratification in exchange for some anticipated greater satisfaction in the future, the more capital goods Crusoe will accumulate and the higher will be his standard of living.

Second, people can increase their wealth through participation in the division of labor. We assume that Crusoe is joined by Friday. Because of their natural, physical, or mental differences or the differences of the "land" (nature) they face, almost automatically absolute and comparative advantages in the production of various goods emerge. Crusoe is better equipped to produce one good and Friday another. If they specialize in what each is particularly good at producing, the total output of goods will be larger than if they had not specialized and remained in a position of an isolated and self-sufficient producer. Alternatively, if either Crusoe or Friday is the superior producer of every good, the all-around superior producer is to specialize in those activities in which his advantage is especially great and the all-around inferior producer must specialize in those activities in which his disadvantage is comparatively smaller. Thereby, too, the overall output of goods produced will be greater than if each had remained in self-sufficient isolation.

Third, the wealth in society depends on the population size, i.e., on whether or not the population is kept at its optimum size. That wealth depends on the population size follows from the "law of returns" and the "Malthusian law of population," which Ludwig von Mises has hailed as

> one of the great achievements of thought. Together with the principle of the division of labor it provided the foundations of modern biology and for the theory of evolution; the importance of these two fundamental theorems for the sciences of human action is second only to the discovery of the regularity in the intertwinement and sequence of market phenomena and their inevitable determination by the market data. The objections raised against the Malthusian law as well as against the law of returns are vain and trivial. Both laws are indisputable.[1]

In its most general and abstract form, the law of returns states that for any combination of two or more production factors there exists an optimum combination (such that any deviation from it involves material waste, or "efficiency losses"). Applied to the two original factors of production, labor and land (nature-given goods), the law implies that if one were to continuously increase the quantity of labor (population) while the quantity of land (and the available technology) remained fixed and unchanged, eventually a point will be reached where the physical output per labor-unit input is

---

[1]Ludwig von Mises, *Human Action: A Treatise on Economics* (Chicago: Regnery, 1966), p. 667.

maximized. This point marks the optimal population size. If the population were to grow beyond this size, income per head would fall; and likewise, income per head would be less if the population were to fall below this point (as the division of labor would shrink, with an accompanying efficiency loss). To maintain the optimal level of income per person, then, the population must no longer grow but remain stationary. Only one way exists for such a stationary society to further increase real income per head or to grow in size without a loss in per capita income: through technological innovation, i.e., by the employment of better, more efficient tools made possible through savings brought about by the abstention from leisure or other immediate consumption. If there is no technological innovation (technology is fixed), the only possible way for the population to grow in size without a concomitant fall in per capita income is through taking more (and possibly better) land into use. If there is no additional land available and technology is fixed at a 'given' level, however, then any population increase beyond the optimal size must lead to a progressive decline in per capita income.

This latter situation has been referred to also as the "Malthusian trap." Ludwig von Mises has characterized it thus:

> The purposive adjustment of the birthrate to the supply of the material potentialities of well-being is an indispensable condition of human life and action, of civilization, and of any improvement in wealth and welfare. ... Where the average standard of living is impaired by the excessive increase in population figures, irreconcilable conflicts of interest arise. Each individual is again a rival of all other individuals in the struggle for survival. The annihilation of rivals is the only means to increase one's well-being. ... As natural conditions are, man has only the choice between the pitiless war of each against each or social cooperation. But social cooperation is

> impossible if people give rein to the natural impulses of proliferation.[2]

It has been already described and explained (in the previous chapter) how all this worked out in hunter-gatherer societies. It is conceivable that mankind had never left the seemingly comfortable hunter-gatherer lifestyle. This would have been possible, if only mankind had been able to restrict all population growth beyond the optimal size of a hunter-gatherer band (of a few dozen members). In that case, we might still live today very much like all of our direct forebears had lived for tens of thousands of years, until some 11,000 or 12,000 years ago. As a matter of fact, however, mankind did not manage to do so. The population did grow, and accordingly increasingly larger territories had to be taken into possession until one ran out of additional land. Moreover, technological advances made within the framework of hunter-gatherer societies (such as the invention of bow and arrow some 20,000 years ago, for instance) increased (rather than decreased) the speed of this expansionism. Because hunters and gatherers (like all nonhuman animals) only depleted (consumed) the supply of nature-given goods, but did not produce and thus add to this supply, better tools in their hands hastened (rather than delayed) the process of territorial expansion.

The Neolithic Revolution, which began about 11,000 years ago, brought some temporary relief. The invention of agriculture and animal husbandry allowed for a larger number of people to survive on the same, unchanged quantity of land, and the institution of the family, in privatizing (inter-

---

[2] Ibid., p. 672.

nalizing) the benefits as well as the costs of the production of offspring, provided a new, hitherto unknown check on the growth of population. But neither innovation brought a permanent solution to the problem of excess population. Men still could not keep their pants up, and the greater productivity brought about by the new, nonparasitic mode of production represented by agriculture and animal husbandry was quickly exhausted again by a growing population size. A significantly larger number of people could be sustained on the globe than before, but mankind did not yet escape from the Malthusian trap — until some 200 years ago with the beginning of the so-called Industrial Revolution.

II. ECONOMIC HISTORY: THE PROBLEM

The problem to be explained in the following has been captured by two charts depicting world population growth on the one hand and the development of per capita income (average living standards) on the other.

The first chart, taken from Colin McEvedy and Richard Jones,[3] shows human population growth from 400 BC until the present (2,000 AD). The population size was about four million at the beginning of the Neolithic Revolution. But up until about 7,000 years ago (5,000 BC) the area under crops (first merely in the region of the Fertile Crescent and then also in northern China) was too small to have much of an effect on the global population size. By then the population had grown to about five million. But since then, population growth increased rapidly: 2,000 years later (3,000 BC) it had

[3]*Atlas of World Population History* (Harmondsworth, U.K.: Penguin Books, 1978), p. 342.

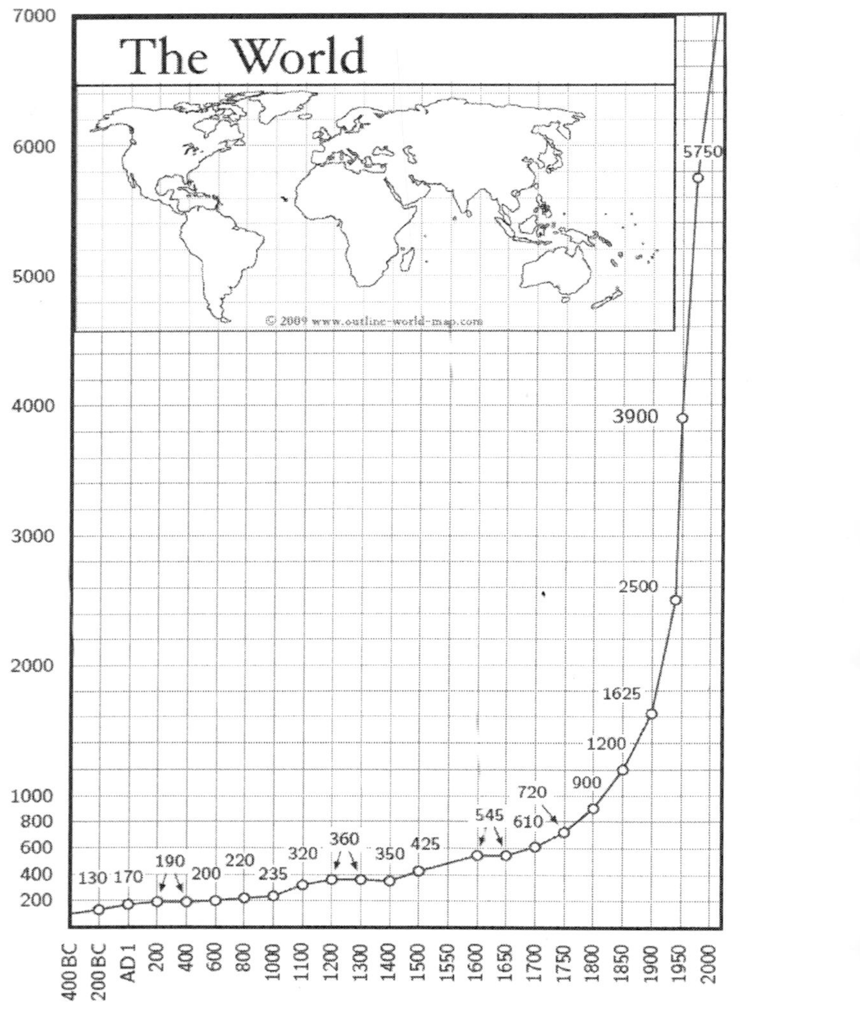

Figure I
Total World Population (millions)
Units — measured in millions of people

almost tripled to fourteen million, 3,000 years ago (1,000 BC) it had reached fifty million,[4] and only some 500 years later, when the chart sets in, the world population size stood at about 100 million. Since then, as the chart indicates, the population size has continued to increase slowly but more or less steadily up until about 1800 (to about 720 million), when a significant break occurred and the population growth sharply increased to presently, only some 200 years later to reach seven billion.

The second chart, taken from Gregory Clark,[5] shows the development of per capita income from the beginning of recorded human history to the present. It too shows a significant break occurring at around 1800. Until that time, i.e., for most of recorded human history, real income per capita (in terms of food, housing, clothing, heating, and lighting) did not rise. That is, average living standards in eighteenth century England were not significantly higher than those in ancient Babylon, where the oldest records of wage rates and various consumer goods prices could be found. Naturally, with sedentary life and private landownership distinct differences in wealth and income came into existence. There existed large landowners (lords) who lived in enormous luxury, even by today's standards, almost from the beginnings of settled life. Nor were average living standards always and everywhere equally low. There existed pronounced regional differences between, for instance, English, Indian, and West African real incomes in 1800. And of course, as far as cross-time comparisons are concerned, many technologies existed

---

[4]Ibid., p. 344.

[5]Gregory Clark, *Farewell to Alms: A Brief Economic History of the World* (Princeton, N.J.: Princeton University Press, 2007), p. 2.

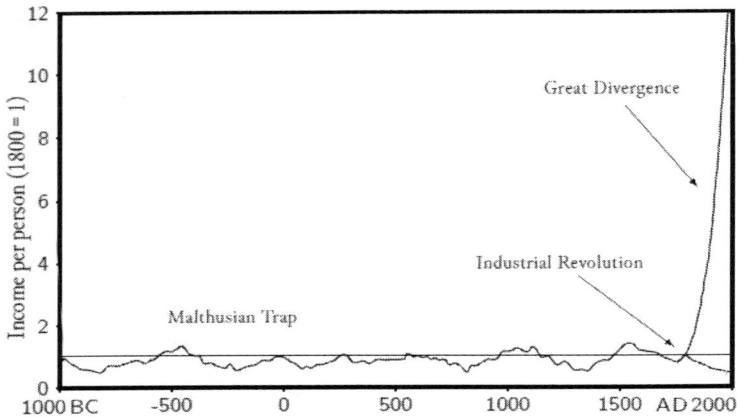

Figure II
World Economic History in One Picture.
Incomes Rose Sharply in Many Countries After 1800 but Declined in Others.

in 1800 England, which were unknown in ancient Rome, Greece, China, or Babylon. Yet in any case, everywhere and at all times the overwhelming majority of the population, the mass of small landowners and most laborers, lived near or only a little bit above subsistence level. There were ups and downs in real incomes, due to various external events, but nowhere was there a continuous upward trend in real income per person discernable until about 1800.

In combination, both charts capture the world-historic significance of the so-called Industrial Revolution, which occurred some 200 years ago, as well as the significance — and in particular the length — of the previous, Malthusian stage of human development. Until sometime around 1800, little difference in the economies of humans and nonhuman animals existed. For animals (and plants) it is always and invariably true that an increase in their number will encroach upon the available means of subsistence and eventually lead to overpopulation, to "supernumerary specimens," as Mises has called them, which must be "weeded out" due to a lack of sustenance. Today, we know that as far as humans are concerned, this *must* not be so: no supernumerary specimens who are thus weeded out exist in modern, western societies. But for most of human life this was indeed the case.

To be sure, the population size could grow, mostly because more land was taken into possession for agricultural use, and partly because of better technology incorporated in producer goods and an extended and intensified division of labor. But all such economic "gains" were always eaten up quickly by a growing population that again encroached upon the available means of subsistence and led to overpopulation and the emergence of the "supernumerary specimen" for whom there was no space in the division of labor and who consequently had to die out silently or become a menace (an economic "bad") in the form of beggars, vagrants, plunderers, bandits, or warriors. Throughout most of human history, then, the iron law of wages held sway. Income and wages were held down near subsistence level owing to the existence of a substantial class of supernumerary specimens.

III. HISTORY EXPLAINED

Why did it take so long to get out of the Malthusian trap; and what happened that we finally succeeded? Why did it take so long until we gave up a hunter-gatherer existence in favor of an existence as agricultural settlers? And why, even after the invention of agriculture and animal husbandry, did it take more than another 10,000 years until mankind's seemingly final escape from the Malthusian trap? Economic theory, or what I have said about it, does not and cannot answer these questions.

The standard answer among economists, in particular also among libertarian economists, is: there must have been institutional impediments, in particular an insufficient protection of private property rights, that prevented a quicker development and these impediments were removed only recently (about 1800). This, essentially, is also Ludwig von Mises's explanation.[6] Likewise, Murray N. Rothbard has advanced similar ideas.[7] I want to argue that this explanation is mistaken or at least insufficient and present the outline of an alternative (hypothetical) explanation.

For one, hunters and gatherers, from all we know, had plenty of free time on their hands to invent agriculture and animal husbandry. Again and again and at countless places, they suffered from excess population and consequently falling incomes; and yet, although the opportunity cost of forgone leisure must have been low, no one anywhere, for tens of thousands of years, thought of agriculture and animal husbandry as an (at least temporary) escape from Malthusian conditions. Instead, until about 11,000 years ago hunter-gatherer tribes answered the recurring challenge of overpopulation always either by migration, i.e., by taking additional land into use (until they finally ran out of land) or by fighting each other to the death until the population size was sufficiently reduced to prevent real incomes from falling.

---

[6]Mises, *Human Action*, pp. 617–23.

[7]Rothbard, "Left and Right," in idem, *Egalitarianism as a Revolt Against Nature and Other Essays* (Auburn, Ala.: Mises Institute, 2000).

As well, property rights in settled societies were well protected at many places and times. The idea of private property and the successful protection of private property are not inventions and institutions of the recent past but have been known for a long time and practiced almost from the beginnings of settled life. From all we know, for instance, property rights in 1200 England and in much of feudal Europe were better protected than they are today in contemporary England and Europe. That is, every institutional incentive favorable to capital accumulation and division of labor was in place — and yet nowhere, until about 1800, did mankind succeed in extricating itself from the Malthusian trap of excess population and stagnating per capita incomes. Thus, the institution of property-protection can and should be regarded as only a necessary, but not also as a sufficient condition of economic growth (rising per capita incomes).

There must be something else — some other factor, not appearing in economic theory — which will have to explain all this.

Part of the answer is obvious: mankind did not get out of the Malthusian trap because, as noted before, men could not keep their pants up. If they had done so, there would have been no excess population. This can be only part of the answer, however. Because population control can prevent the fall of real incomes, but it cannot make incomes rise.[8] Some other,

---

[8]When Tahiti was rediscovered by Europeans in 1767, some 1,000 or possibly 2,000 years after it had been first settled by Austronesian farmers, its population was estimated at 50,000 (today, 180,000). According to all accounts, the Tahitians lived paradisiacal lives. Real income per capita was high, not least because of highly favorable climatic conditions in the Polynesian islands. Tahitian men could not

"empirical" factor not figuring in pure (aprioristic) economic theory must explain the length of the Malthusian age and how we finally got out of it. This missing factor is the historical *variable* of human intelligence, and the simple answer to the above questions, then, (to be elaborated in the following) is: because for most of history mankind was simply not intelligent enough — and it takes time to breed intelligence.[9]

Until some 11,000 or so years ago, mankind was not intelligent enough, such that not even its brightest members were capable of conceiving the idea of indirect or roundabout consumer goods production that underlies agriculture and animal husbandry. The idea of first planting crops, then tending and protecting and finally harvesting them is not obvious or trivial. Nor is the idea of taming, husbanding, and breeding animals obvious or trivial. It requires a considerable degree of intelligence to conceive of such notions. It took tens of thousands of years of natural selection under hunter-gatherer conditions to finally breed enough intelligence to make such cognitive achievements possible.

---

keep their pants up either, but in order to maintain their high standard of living, the Tahitians practiced a most rigorous and ruthless form of population control, involving infanticide and deadly warfare. The place was paradise, but a paradise only for the living. Yet all the while Tahitians were still living in the Stone Age. Their tool kit had remained essentially unchanged since their first arrival on the island(s). There had been no further capital accumulation, and real income per capita, even if high due to favorable external circumstances, had remained stagnant.

[9]See Michael H. Hart, *Understanding Human History: An Analysis Including the Effects of Geography and Differential Evolution* (Augusta, Ga.: Washington Summit Publishers, 2007).

Similarly, it took several thousand years more of natural selection under agricultural conditions, then, to reach a threshold in the development of human intelligence (or more precisely: of low time preference correlated with high intelligence) such that productivity growth could continuously outstrip any population growth. From the beginning of the Neolithic Revolution until about 1800 enough inventions (technological improvements) were made by bright people (and imitated by others of lesser intelligence) to account (in addition to more agriculturally used land) for a significant increase in world population: from about four million to 720 million (now, seven billion). But during the entire era, the rate of technological progress was never sufficient to allow for population growth *combined* with increasing per capita incomes.

Today, we take it for granted that it is solely the unwillingness to consume less and to save more that imposes limits on economic growth. We have a seemingly endless supply of natural resources and recipes how to produce more, better, and different goods, and it is only our limited savings that prevent us from employing these resources and implement such recipes. Yet this phenomenon is actually quite new. For most of human history savings were held back by a lack of ideas of how to productively invest them, i.e., of how to convert plain savings (storing) into productive savings (producer goods production). For Crusoe, for instance, it was not sufficient to have a low time preference and to save. Rather, Crusoe also had to conceive the idea of a net and must have known how to build it from scratch. Most people are not intelligent enough to invent and implement anything new but can at best only imitate, more or less perfectly, what other, brighter people have invented before them. Yet if no one is capable to do this or to imitate what others have invented before, then even the safest of property rights will make no difference. Every incentive needs a receptor to work, and if a receptor is lacking or insufficiently sensitive, different incentive structures do not matter. Hence, the institution of property-protection must be regarded as only a necessary (but not sufficient) condition of economic growth (rising per capita incomes). Likewise, it requires intelligence to recognize the higher physical productivity of the division of labor, and it requires intelligence to recognize the laws of human reproduction and thus allow for any form of deliberate population control, let alone an efficient — low-cost — control.

The mechanism through which higher human intelligence (combined with low time preference) was bred over time is straightforward. Given that man is physically weak and ill-equipped to deal with brute nature, it was advantageous for him to develop his intelligence.[10] Higher intelligence translated into economic success, and economic success in turn translated into reproductive success (producing a larger number of surviving descendants). For the existence of both relationships massive amounts of empirical evidence are available.[11]

There can be no doubt that a hunter-gatherer existence requires intelligence: the ability to classify various external objects as good or bad, the ability to recognize a multiplicity of causes and effects, to estimate distances, time, and speed,

---

[10]See also Arnold Gehlen, *Man* (New York: Columbia University Press, 1988).

[11]See also Hart, *Understanding Human History*; Clark, *Farewell to Alms*, chap. 6; and Richard Lynn, *Dysgenics: Genetic Deterioration in Modern Populations* (Ulster: Ulster Institute for Social Research, 2011), chap. 2.

to survey and recognize landscapes, to locate various (good or bad) things and to remember their position in relation to each other, etc.; most importantly, the ability to communicate with others by means of language and thus facilitate coordination. Not every member of a band was equally capable of such skills. Some were more intelligent than others. These differences in intellectual talents would lead to some visible status differentiation within the tribe — of "excellent" hunters, gatherers, and communicators and "lousy" ones — and this status differentiation would in turn result in differences in the reproductive success of various tribe members, especially given the "loose" sexual mores prevailing among hunter-gatherers. That is, by and large "excellent" tribe members would produce a larger number of surviving offspring and thus transmit their genes more successfully into the next generation than "lousy" ones. Consequently, if and insofar as human intelligence has some genetic basis (which seems undeniable in light of the evolution of the entire species), hunter-gatherer conditions would over time produce (select for) a population of increasing average intelligence and at the same time an increasingly higher level of "exceptional" intelligence.

The competition within and between tribes, and the selection for and breeding of higher intelligence via differential rates of reproductive success, did not come to a halt once the hunter-gatherer life had been given up in favor of agriculture and animal husbandry. However, the intellectual requirements of economic success became somewhat different under sedentary conditions.

The invention of agriculture and animal husbandry was in and of itself an outstanding cognitive achievement. It required a lengthened planning horizon. It required longer provisions and deeper and farther-reaching insights into the chains of natural causes and effects. And it required more work, patience, and endurance than under hunter-gatherer conditions. In addition, it was instrumental for success as a farmer that one possessed some degree of numeracy so as to count, measure, and proportion. It required intelligence to recognize the advantages of interhousehold division of labor and to abandon self-sufficiency. It required some literacy to design contracts and establish contractual relations. And it required some skill of monetary calculation and of accountancy to economically succeed. Not every farmer was equally apt in these skills and had an equally low degree of time preference. To the contrary, under agricultural conditions, where each household was responsible for its own production of consumer goods and offspring and there was no longer any "free riding" as under hunter-gatherer conditions, the natural inequality of man, and the corresponding social differentiation of and between more or less successful members of a tribe became increasingly and strikingly visible (in particular through the size of one's land holdings). Consequently, the translation of economic (productive) success and status into reproductive success, i.e., the breeding of a comparatively larger number of surviving offspring by the economically successful, became even more direct and pronounced.

Further, this tendency of selecting for higher intelligence would be particularly pronounced under "harsh" external conditions. If the human environment is unchangingly constant and "mild" — as in the season-less tropics, where one day is like another year in and out — high or exceptional intelligence offers a lesser advantage than in an inhospitable environment with widely fluctuating seasonal variations. The more challenging the environment, the higher the premium placed on intelligence as a requirement of economic, and consequently reproductive success. Hence, the growth of human intelligence would be most pronounced in harsher (historically, generally northern) regions of human habitation.

Humans live on — consume — animals and plants, and animals live on other animals or plants. Plants, thus, stand at the beginning of the human food chain. The growth of plants in turn depends on the presence (or absence) of four factors: carbon dioxide (which is evenly distributed across the globe and hence of no interest here), solar energy, water, and, very importantly, minerals (such as potassium, phosphates, etc.).[12]

At the equator, where (nearby) the first modern humans lived, two of the three conditions of biological growth were met perfectly. There existed an abundance of sunlight and of rain. Rain fell predictably almost daily. Days and nights were equally long and temperatures year-round comfortably warm, with little to no difference between day vs. night and summer vs. winter temperatures. In the tropical rainforest, temperatures rarely exceed 30 degrees Celsius (86 degrees Fahrenheit) and rarely fall below 20 degrees Celsius (68 degrees Fahrenheit). Winds were generally calm, interrupted only by sudden brief storms. The conditions for human habitation, then, would appear quite appealing; and yet, the population density in tropical regions is and has always been extremely low as compared to that in regions further north (and south), sometimes, as in the rainforests of the Amazon, nearly as low as the population density typical of deserts or

---

[12]See on the following Josef H. Reichholf, *Stabile Ungleichgewichte: Die Ökologie der Zukunft* (Frankfurt: Suhrkamp, 2008); also Carroll Quigley, *The Evolution of Civilizations: An Introduction to Historical Analysis* (Indianapolis: Liberty Classics, 1979), chap. 6.

arctic regions. The reason for this is the extreme shortage of soil minerals in the tropics.

The soil of the tropics is, geologically speaking, old (as compared in particular to those regions affected by the earth-historical sequence of glacial and interglacial periods) and almost completely drained of minerals (except for equatorial regions with volcanic — mineral producing — activity as on some Indonesian islands such as Java, for instance, where the human population density has in fact always been significantly higher). As a result, the enormous biomass characteristic of the tropics produces no new, surplus or excess growth. Growth is year-round, but it is slow, and it does not lead to an increase in the total biomass. Once grown up, the rainforest only recycles itself. Moreover, the overwhelming proportion of this biomass is in the form of slow growing hardwood trees, i.e., of dead matter; and the leaves of most tropical plants, due to their peculiar need for protection (cooling) against the intense equator sun, are not only hard and tough but often poisonous or at least distasteful to humans and other plant-eaters such as cattle and deer. This absence of surplus growth and the special chemistry of tropical plants explains the fact that, contrary to what is frequently imagined, the tropics support only amazingly few and smallish animals. Indeed, the only animals existing in abundance are ants and termites. A tropical biomass (mostly of wood) of more than 1,000 tons per hectare produces no more than 200 kilograms of meat (animal mass), i.e., one-five-thousandth of the plant mass. (In contrast, in the East African grassland savannah a mere fifty tons of plant mass per square kilometer (100 hectare) produces some twenty tons of animal mass: of elephants, buffalos, zebras, gnus, antelopes, and gazelles.) Yet where there are so few and nonsizeable animals, only few humans can be sustained. (In fact, most people who lived in the tropics lived near rivers and sustained their lives essentially from fishing rather than hunting and gathering).

At their place of origin, then, humans very quickly arrived at the point where they had to leave the paradisiacal, warm, stable, and predictable environment of the tropics and enter other regions in search of food. The regions northward (and southward) of the equator were seasonal regions, however. That is, they had less, and less constant rainfall than the tropics, and the temperatures increasingly fell and varied more widely as one moved northward (or southward). In northern regions of human habitation, temperatures could easily vary by more than 40 degrees per day and seasonal temperatures by more than 80 degrees. The total biomass produced under such conditions was significantly less than in the tropics. However, further away from the equator the soil had (often) sufficient or even ample minerals to compensate for these climatic disadvantages and offered optimal conditions for the growth of vegetation suited for animal and human consumption: of plants that grew fast and, in spurts, produced large seasonal surpluses of fresh biomass — in particular of grasses (including grains) — that could support a large number of sizable animals.

During the last ice age, which ended some 10,000 years ago, the regions which offered this less than paradisiacal climatic conditions but a superior food supply included (concentrating here on the northern hemisphere, where most of the considered development took place) all of supra-equatorial Africa — including the Sahara — and most of the Eurasian land mass (except for still-arctic northern Europe and Siberia). Since then, and essentially continuing until today, a northern belt of deserts, which widens toward the east, has come to separate the entire zone of seasonal regions into a southern one of subequatorial regions and a northern one that includes now also most of northern Europe and Siberia. From the hunter-gatherer stage of human development essentially until today, then, the highest population density could be found in these "moderate" seasonal regions (a picture further modified only by altitudes).

It is important to realize in this context, however, that what we have come to regard as "moderate" regions of human habitation were actually quite harsh living conditions, and in far northern latitudes even extremely harsh conditions as compared to those in the constantly warm tropics, to which humans first had been adapted. In contrast to the stable and unchanging environment of the tropics, moderate regions presented increased change and fluctuation and thus posed (increasingly) difficult intellectual challenges to hunters and gatherers. Not only did they have to learn how to deal with large animals, which did not exist in the tropics (except for the volcanic parts of Indonesia), and their movements. More importantly, outside equatorial regions seasonal changes and fluctuations in the human environment played an increasingly greater role, and it became increasingly important to predict such changes and fluctuations and to anticipate their effects on the future food supply (of plants and animals). Those who could do so successfully and make appropriate preparations and adjustments, had a better chance of survival and proliferation than those who could not.

Outside the equatorial rainforest, to the north (and south), pronounced raining seasons existed and had to be taken into account. It rained during the summer and was dry in the winter. As well, the growth and distribution of plants and animals was affected by northeasterly (or, in the southern hemisphere, southeasterly) trade winds. In regions still further to the north (or south), increasingly separated since the end of the last ice age from the subequatorial regions by a belt of (northern and southern) deserts, the rain seasons shifted, with rain in the winter and drought in the summer. The winds affecting the distribution of rain were prevailingly westerlies. Summers were hot and dry, while winter temperatures, even in low altitudes, could easily reach "deadly" freezing levels, even if only for short periods. Growing seasons were accordingly limited. Lastly, in the northernmost regions of human habitation, i.e., north of Mediterranean latitudes, rain fell irregularly throughout the year and, with prevailing westerly winds, more in the west (northern Europe) than in the east (northern Asia). Otherwise, however, seasonal changes and fluctuations in this zone of human habitation were extreme. The lengths of days (light) and nights (dark) varied remarkably throughout the year. In extreme northern regions, a light summer day and a dark winter night both could last for more than a month. More importantly, the entire region (and especially pronounced as one moved in a northeasterly direction) experienced extended periods of often extreme freezing conditions during the winter. During these periods, lasting from many months to most of the year, all plant growth came essentially to a standstill. Plants died or went dormant. Nature stopped supplying food, and humans (and animals) were threatened with starvation and the danger of freezing to death. The growing seasons, during which a surplus of food and shelter could possibly be built up for this contingency, were accordingly short. Moreover, the extreme differences between long, harsh, and freezing winters and the short, mild to warm growing seasons, affected the migration of animals. Unless they had fully adapted to arctic conditions and could go into some form of hibernation during "dead" seasons, animals had to migrate from season to season, often over long distances to and from far apart locations. And since animals constituted a major part of the human food supply, hunter-gatherers, too, had to migrate regularly over large distances.

Before the background of this rough picture of human ecology and geography, further modified and complicated of course by the existence of mountain ranges, rivers, and bodies of water, it becomes apparent why the natural selection in favor of higher intelligence among hunter-gatherers would be more pronounced as one moved in a northern (or southern) direction toward the coldest regions of human habitation. No doubt, significant intelligence was required of humans to live successfully in the tropics. However, the equilibrium-like constancy of the tropics acted as a natural constraint on the further development of human intelligence. Because one day was much like any other day in the tropics, little or no need existed for anyone to take anything into account in his actions except his immediate surroundings or to plan beyond anything but the immediately impending future. In distinct contrast, the increasing seasonality of regions outside the tropics made for an intellectually increasingly challenging environment.

The existence of seasonal changes and fluctuations — of rain and drought, summer and winter, scorching heat and freezing cold, winds and calms — required that more, and more remote factors including the sun, the moon, and the stars, and longer stretches of time had to be taken into account if one wanted to act successfully and survive and procreate. More and longer chains of causes and effects had to be recognized and more and longer chains of argument thought through. The planning horizon had to be extended in time. One had to act now, in order to be successful much later.

Both the period of production — the time lapse between the onset of a productive effort and its completion — and the period of provision — the time span into the future for which present provisions (savings) had to be made — needed to be lengthened. In the northernmost regions, with long and deadly winters, provisions of food, clothing, shelter, and heating had to be made that would last through most of a year or beyond. Planning had to be in terms of years, instead of days or months. As well, in pursuit of seasonally and widely migrating animals, extensive territories had to be traversed, requiring exceptional skills of orientation and navigation. Only groups intelligent enough on average to generate exceptional leaders who possessed such superior intellectual skills and abilities were rewarded with success — survival and procreation. Those groups and leaders, on the other hand, who were not capable of these achievements, were punished with failure, i.e., extinction.

The greatest progress on the way toward the invention of agriculture and animal husbandry some 11,000 years ago, then, should have occurred in the northernmost regions of human habitation. Here, the competition within and between hunter-gatherer groups should have produced over time the most intelligent — provisionary and farsighted — population. And indeed, during the tens of thousands of years until about 11,000 years ago, every significant technological advance originated in northern regions: mostly in Europe or, in the case of ceramics, in Japan. In contrast, during the same period the toolkit used in the tropics remained almost unchanged.

But the explanatory power of the above sketch of social evolution goes much further. The admittedly hypothetical theory presented here can explain why it took so long to get out of the Malthusian trap, and how such a feat was possible at all and we did not remain under Malthusian conditions forever: Mankind was simply not intelligent enough to achieve productivity increases that could continuously outstrip population growth. A certain threshold of average and exceptional intelligence had to be reached first for this to become possible, and it took time (until about 1800) to "breed" such a level of intelligence. The theory can explain the well-established and corroborated (and yet for "political correctness" reasons persistently ignored) fact of intelligence research: that the average IQ of nations gradually declines as one moves from north to south (from about 100 or more points in northern countries to about seventy in sub-Saharan Africa).[13] More specifically, the theory can thus explain why the Industrial Revolution originated and then took hold immediately in some — generally northern — regions but not in others, why there had always existed persistent regional income differences, and why these differences could have increased (rather than decreased) since the time of the Industrial Revolution.

As well, the theory can explain what may at first appear as an anomaly: that it was not in the northernmost regions of human habitation where the Neolithic Revolution began some 11,000 years ago and whence it gradually and successively conquered the rest of the world, but in regions significantly further south — yet still far north of the tropics: in the

---

[13]See Richard Lynn & Tatu Vanhanen, *IQ and Global Inequality* (Augusta, Ga.: Washington Summit Publishers, 2006); Richard Lynn, *The Global Bell Curve: Race, IQ and Inequality Worldwide* (Augusta, Ga.: Washington Summit Publishers, 2008); idem, *Race Differences in Intelligence: An Evolutionary Analysis* (Augusta Ga.: Washington Summit Publishers, 2008).

Middle East, in central China (the Yangtze Valley), and in Mesoamerica. The reason for this seeming anomaly is easy to detect, however. In order to invent agriculture and animal husbandry two factors were necessary: sufficient intelligence and favorable natural circumstances to apply such intelligence. It was the second factor that was lacking in extreme northern regions and thus prevented its inhabitants from making the revolutionary invention. The extreme freezing conditions and the extreme brevity of the growing season there made agriculture and animal husbandry practically impossible, even if the idea might have been conceived. What was necessary to actually implement the idea were natural circumstances favorable to sedentary life: of a long and warm growing season (besides suitable crops, and domesticable animals).[14] Such climatic conditions existed in the mentioned "temperate" regions. Here, the competitive development of human intelligence among hunter-gatherers had made sufficient progress (even if it lagged behind that in the north) so that, combined with favorable natural circumstances, the idea of agriculture and animal husbandry could be implemented. Since the end of the last ice age about 10,000 years ago, then, the zone of temperate climates expanded northward into higher latitudes, rendering agriculture and animal husbandry increasingly feasible there as well. Meeting there an even more intelligent people, the new revolutionary production techniques were not merely quickly imitated and adopted, but most subsequent improvements in these techniques had its origins here. South of the centers of the original invention, too, the new

[14]The greater scarcity of such crops and animals on the American continent is the likely reason for the somewhat belated third independent invention of agriculture and animal husbandry in Mesoamerica.

technique would be gradually adopted (with the exception of the tropics) — after all, it is easier to imitate something than to invent it. Meeting a less intelligent people there, however, little or no contribution to the further development of more efficient practices of agriculture or animal husbandry would come from there. All further efficiency gains in these regions would stem from the imitation of techniques invented elsewhere, in regions further north.

IV. IMPLICATIONS AND OUTLOOK

Several implications and suggestions follow from this. First, the theory of social evolution sketched here entails a fundamental criticism of the egalitarianism rampant within the social sciences generally but also among many libertarians. True, economists allow for human "differences" in the form of different labor productivities. But these differences are generally interpreted as the result of different external conditions, i.e., of different endowments or training. Only rarely are internal, biologically anchored characteristics admitted as possible sources of human differences. Yet even when economists admit the obvious: that human differences have internal, biological sources as well, as Mises and Rothbard certainly do, they still typically ignore that these differences are themselves in turn the outcome of a lengthy process of natural selection in favor of human characteristics and dispositions (physical and mental) determinant of economic success and, more or less highly positively correlated with economic success, of reproductive success. That is, it is still largely overlooked that we, modern man, are a very different breed from our predecessors hundreds or even thousands of years ago.

Second, once it is realized that the Industrial Revolution was first and foremost the outcome of the evolutionary growth of human intelligence (rather than the mere removal of institutional barriers to growth), the role of the State can be recognized as fundamentally different under Malthusian vs. post-Malthusian conditions. Under Malthusian conditions the State doesn't matter much, at least as far as macro-effects are concerned. A more exploitative State will simply lead to a lower population number (much like a pest would), but it does not affect per capita income. In fact, in lowering the population density, income per capita may even rise, as it did after the great pestilence in the mid-fourteenth century. And in reverse: a "good," less-exploitative State will allow for a growing number of people, but per capita incomes will not rise or may even fall, because land per capita is reduced. All this changes with the Industrial Revolution. For if productivity gains continuously outstrip population increases and allow for a steady increase in per capita incomes, then an exploitative institution such as the State can continuously grow without lowering per capita income and reducing the population number. The State then becomes a permanent drag on the economy and per capita incomes.

Third, whereas under Malthusian conditions positive eugenic effects reign: the economically successful produce more surviving offspring and the population stock is thus gradually bettered (cognitively improved). Under post-Malthusian conditions the existence and the growth of the State produces a two-fold dysgenic effect, especially under democratic welfare-state conditions.[15] For one, the "economically challenged," as the principal "clients" of the welfare State,

[15]Lynn, *Dysgenics*.

produce more surviving offspring, and the economically successful less. Second, the steady growth of a parasitic State, made possible by a growing underlying economy, systematically affects the requirements of economic success. Economic success becomes increasingly dependent on politics and political talent, i.e., the talent of using the State to enrich oneself at others' expense. In any case, the population stock becomes increasingly worse (as far as the cognitive requirements of prosperity and economic growth are concerned), rather than better.

Finally, it is important to note in conclusion, then, that just as the Industrial Revolution and the attendant escape from the Malthusian trap was by no means a necessary development in human history so its success and achievements are also not irreversible.

3

FROM ARISTOCRACY TO MONARCHY TO DEMOCRACY

IN THE FOLLOWING I WANT TO BRIEFLY describe a historical puzzle or riddle that I will then try to solve and answer in some detail.

But before that, it is necessary to make a few brief general theoretical observations.

Men do not live in perfect harmony with each other. Rather, again and again conflicts arise between them. And the source of these conflicts is always the same: the scarcity of goods. I want to do *X* with a given good *G* and you want to do simultaneously *Y* with the very same good. Because it is impossible for you and me to do simultaneously *X* and *Y* with *G*, you and I must clash. If a superabundance of goods existed, i.e., if, for instance, *G* were available in unlimited supply, our conflict could be avoided. We could both simultaneously do 'our thing' with *G*. But most goods do not exist in superabundance. Ever since mankind left the Garden of Eden, there has been and always will be scarcity all-around us.

Absent a perfect harmony of all human interests and given the permanent human condition of scarcity, then, interpersonal conflicts are an inescapable part of human life and a constant threat to peace.

Confronted with conflicts concerning scarce goods, but also endowed with reason or more precisely with the ability to communicate, to discuss and to argue with one another, as the very manifestation of human reason, then, mankind has been and forever will be faced with the question of how to possibly avoid such conflicts and how to peacefully resolve them should they occur.[1]

Assume now a group of people aware of the reality of interpersonal conflicts and in search of a way out of this predicament. And assume that I then propose the following as a solution: In every case of conflict, including conflicts in which I myself am involved, I will have the last and final word. I will be the ultimate judge as to who owns what and when and who is accordingly right or wrong in any

[1]Theoretically, all conflicts regarding the use of any good can be avoided, if only every good is always and continuously privately owned, i.e., exclusively controlled, by some specified individual(s) and it is always clear which thing is owned, and by whom, and which is not. The interests and ideas of different individuals may then be as different as can be, and yet no conflict arises, insofar as their interests and ideas are concerned always and exclusively with their own, separate property. Conflicts, then, are always conflicts regarding the answer to the question as to who is or is not the private (exclusive) owner of any given good at any given time. And in order to avoid all conflicts from the beginning of mankind on, it must be further always clear how private property is originally established (and here the obvious answer is: by original and thus undisputed appropriation of previously unowned resources) and how property then can or cannot be transferred from one person to another (obviously: by mutual consent and trading rather than unilateral robbery).

dispute regarding scarce resources. This way, all conflicts can be avoided or smoothly resolved.

What would be my chances of finding your or anyone else's agreement to this proposal?

My guess is that my chances would be virtually zero, nil. In fact, you and most people will think of this proposal as ridiculous and likely consider me crazy, a case for psychiatric treatment. For you will immediately realize that under this proposal you must literally fear for your life and property. Because this solution would allow me to cause or provoke a conflict with you and then decide this conflict in my own favor. Indeed, under this proposal you would essentially give up your right to life and property or even any pretense to such a right. You have a right to life and property only insofar as I *grant* you such a right, i.e., as long as I decide to let you live and keep whatever you consider yours. Ultimately, only I have a right to life and I am the owner of all goods.

And yet — and here is the puzzle — this obviously crazy solution is the *reality*. Wherever you look, it has been put into effect in the form of the institution of a State. The State is the ultimate judge in every case of conflict. There is no appeal beyond its verdicts. If you get into conflicts with the State, with its agents, it is the State and its agents who decide who is right and who is wrong. The State has the right to *tax* you. Thereby, it is the State that makes the decision how much of your property you are allowed to keep — that is, your property is only "fiat" property. And the State can *make* laws, legislate — that is, your entire life is at the mercy of the State. It can even order that you be killed — not in defense of your own life and property but in the defense of the State or whatever the State considers "defense" of its "state-property."

How, then, and this is the question I want to address at some length now, could such a wondrous, indeed crazy institution come into existence? Obviously, it could not have developed *ab ovo*, spontaneously, as the outcome of rational human deliberation. In fact, historically, it took centuries for this to happen. In the following I want to reconstruct this development in a step-by-step fashion: from the beginnings of a natural, aristocratic social order as it was approached, for instance, although still riddled with many imperfections, during the early European Middle Ages of feudal kings and lords, to and through its successive displacement by first absolute and then constitutional kings and classic monarchies, which took historic stage from about the seventeenth century on until the early twentieth century, and lastly to and through the successive displacement and final replacement of classic monarchies by democracies (parliamentary republics or monarchies), beginning with the French Revolution and coming into full swing with the end of World War I, since 1918.

While we have learned in school to regard this entire development as progress — no wonder, because history is always written by its victors — I will reconstruct it here as a tale of progressive folly and decay. And to immediately answer a question that will invariably arise in view of this, my revisionist account of history: Yes, the present world is richer than people were in the Middle Ages and the following monarchical age. But that does not show that it is richer *because* of this development. As a matter of fact, as I will demonstrate indirectly in the following, the increase in social wealth and general standards of living that mankind has experienced during this time occurred *in spite* of this development, and the increase of wealth and living standards would have been far greater if the development in question had *not* taken place.

Again, then: How would real, rational, peace-seeking people have solved the problem of social conflict? And let me emphasize the word "real" here. The people I have in mind, deliberating on this question, are not zombies. They do not sit behind a "veil of ignorance," *à la* Rawls, unconstrained by scarcity and time. (No wonder Rawls reached the most perverse conclusions from such a premise!) They stand in the middle of life, so to speak, when they begin their deliberations. They are only too familiar with the inescapable fact of scarcity and of time-constraints. They already work and produce. They interact with other workers and producers, and they have already many goods appropriated and put under their physical control, i.e., taken into possession. Indeed, their disputes are invariably disputes about previously undisputed possessions: whether these are to be further respected and the possessor is to be regarded their rightful owner or not.

What people would most likely accept as a solution, then, I suggest, is this: Everyone is, first-off or prima facie, presumed to be the owner — endowed with the right of exclusive control — of all those goods that he already, in fact, and so far undisputed, controls and possesses. This is the starting point. As their possessor, he has, prima facie, a better claim to the things in question than anyone else who does not control and does not possess these goods — and consequently, if someone else interferes with the possessor's control of such goods, then this person is prima facie in the wrong and the burden of proof, that is to show otherwise, is on him. However, as this last qualification already shows, present possession is not sufficient to be in the right. There is a presumption in favor of the first, actual possessor, and the demonstration of who has actual control or who took first control of something stands always at the beginning of an attempt at conflict resolution (because, to reiterate, every conflict is a conflict between someone who already controls something and someone else who wants to do so instead). But there are exceptions to this rule. The actual possessor of a good is not its rightful owner, if someone else can demonstrate that the good in question had been previously controlled by him and was taken away from him against his will and consent — that it was stolen or robbed from him — by the current possessor. If he can demonstrate this, then ownership reverts back to him and in the conflict between him and the actual possessor he is judged to be in the right. And the current possessor of some thing is likewise not its owner, if he has only rented the thing in question from someone else for some time and under some stated conditions and this other person can demonstrate this fact by presenting, for instance, a prior rental contract or agreement. And the current possessor of a thing is also not its owner if he worked on behalf of someone else, as his employee, to use or produce the good in question and the employer can demonstrate this to be the fact by, for instance, presenting an employment contract.[2]

The criteria, the principles, employed in deciding a conflict between a present controller and possessor of something and the rival claims of another person to control the same thing are clear then, and it can be safely assumed that universal agreement among real people can and will be reached regarding them. What is lacking in actual conflicts, then, is not the absence of law, lawlessness, but only the absence of an agreement on the facts. And the need for judges and conflict

[2]It should be noted that the logical requirements for permanent peace, for the potential avoidance of all conflicts, are met precisely with this solution. It is always clear who provisionally owns what and what to do if rival claims regarding scarce resources exist.

arbitrators, then, is not a need for law-making, but a need for fact-finding and the application of given law to individual cases and specific situations. Put somewhat differently: the deliberations will result in the insight that laws are not to be made but given to be discovered, and that the task of the judge is only and exclusively that of applying given law to established or to be established facts.

Assuming then a demand on the part of conflicting parties for specialized judges, arbitrators, and peacemakers, not to make law but to apply given law, to whom will people turn to satisfy this demand? Obviously, they will not turn to just anyone, because most people do not have the intellectual ability or the character necessary to make for a quality judge and most people's words, then, have no authority and little if any chance of being listened to, respected and enforced. Instead, in order to settle their conflicts and to have the settlement lastingly recognized and respected by others, they will turn to natural authorities, to members of the natural aristocracy, to nobles and kings.

What I mean by natural aristocrats, nobles and kings here is simply this: In every society of some minimum degree of complexity, a few individuals acquire the status of a natural elite. Due to superior achievements of wealth, wisdom, bravery, or a combination thereof, some individuals come to possess more authority than others and their opinion and judgment commands widespread respect. Moreover, because of selective mating and the laws of civil and genetic inheritance, positions of natural authority are often passed on within a few "noble" families. It is to the heads of such families with established records of superior achievement, farsightedness and exemplary conduct that men typically turn with their conflicts and complaints against each other. It is the leaders of the noble families who generally act as judges and peacemakers, often free of charge, out of a sense of civic duty. In fact, this phenomenon can still be observed today, in every small community.

Now back to the question as to the likely outcome of a deliberation among real people about how to resolve the ineradicable human problem of interpersonal conflicts. We can easily imagine, for instance, that there will be general agreement that in every case of conflict one will turn to some specific individual, to the head of the most noble of families, a king. But as already indicated, it is unimaginable that there will be agreement that this king can *make* laws. The king will be held to be under and bound by the same law as everyone else. The king is supposed to only apply law, not make it. And to assure this, the king will never be granted a monopoly on his position as judge. It might be the case that everyone does in fact turn to him for justice, i.e., that he has a 'natural' monopoly as ultimate judge and peacemaker. But everyone remains free to select another judge, another noble, if he is dissatisfied with the king. The king has no legal monopoly on his position as judge, that is. If he is found to make law, instead of just applying it, or if he is found to commit errors in the application of law, i.e., if he misconstrues, misrepresents, or falsifies the facts of a given case, his judgment stands open to be challenged in another noble court of justice, and he himself can there be held liable for his misjudgment. In short, the king may look like the head of a State, but he definitely is not a State but instead part of a natural, vertically and hierarchically structured and stratified social order: an aristocracy.

As I already indicated before, something like this, something resembling an aristocratic natural order had come into existence, for instance, during the early European Middle Ages, during the much-maligned feudal age. Since it is not my purpose here to engage in standard history, i.e., history as it is written by historians, but to offer a logical or sociological reconstruction of history, informed by actual historical events, but motivated more fundamentally by theoretical — philosophical and economic — concerns, I will not spend much time to prove this thesis. I simply refer summarily to a book on this subject by Fritz Kern, *Kingship and Law in the Middle Ages* (originally published in German in 1914), and to numerous other references given to this effect in my book *Democracy: The God That Failed.* Only this much on the allegedly "dark" age of feudalism and in support of my assertion that the Middle Ages can serve as a rough historical example of what I have just described as a natural order.

Feudal lords and kings could only "tax" with the consent of the taxed, and on his own land, every free man was as much of a sovereign, i.e., the ultimate decision maker, as the feudal king was on his. Without consent, taxation was considered sequestration, i.e., unlawful expropriation. The king was below and subordinate to the law. The king might be a noble, even the noblest person of all, but there were other nobles and not-so-nobles, and all of them, every noble and every free man no less or more than the king himself was subordinate to the same law and bound to protect and uphold this law. This law was considered ancient and eternal. "New" laws were routinely rejected as not laws at all. The sole function of the medieval king was that of applying and protecting "good old law." The idea of kingship by birthright was absent during early medieval times. To become king required the consent of those doing the choosing, and every member and every section of the community of electors was free to resist the king if it deemed his actions unlawful. In that case, people were free to abandon the king and seek out a new one.

This brief description of the feudal order or more specifically "allodial" feudalism shall suffice for my purpose. Let me only add this. I do not claim here that this order was perfect, a true natural order, as I have characterized it before. In fact, it was marred by many imperfections, most notably the existence, at many places, of the institution of serfdom (although the burden imposed on serfs then was mild compared to that imposed on today's modern tax-serfs). I only claim that this order approached a natural order through (a) the supremacy of and the subordination of everyone under *one* law, (b) the absence of any law-*making* power, and (c) the lack of any legal *monopoly* of judgeship and conflict arbitration. And I would claim that this system could have been perfected and retained virtually unchanged through the inclusion of serfs into the system.

But this is not what happened. Instead, a fundamental moral and economic folly was committed. A territorial monopoly of ultimate judgeship was established and with this the power of law-*making*, and the separation of law from and its subordination to *legislation*. Feudal kings were replaced first by absolute and then by constitutional kings.

Conceptually, the step from a feudal king under the law to an absolute king above the law is a small one. The formerly feudal king only insists that henceforth no one may rightfully choose anyone else but himself as ultimate judge. Until then, the king might have been the only person to whom everyone turned for justice, but others, other nobles in particular, could have acted as judges if only they had wanted to do so and there had been a demand for such services on the part of justice-seekers. Indeed, everyone had been free to engage in self-defense of his person and property and in private self-adjudication and conflict resolution, and the king himself could be held accountable and brought to justice in other courts of justice, i.e., courts not of his own choosing. To prohibit all this and insist instead that all conflicts be subject to final royal review, then, is no less than a coup, with momentous consequences. As already indicated before, with the monopolization of the function of ultimate judge, the king had become a State and private property had been essentially abolished and replaced by *fiat* property, i.e., by property granted by the king to his subjects. The king could now tax private property instead of having to ask private property owners for subsidies, and he could make laws instead of being bound by unchangeable pre-existing laws. Consequently, slowly but surely law and law enforcement became more expensive: instead of being offered free of charge or for a voluntary payment, they were financed with the help of a compulsory tax. At the same time, the quality of law deteriorated: Instead of upholding pre-existing law and applying universal and immutable principles of justice, the king, as a monopolistic judge who did not have to fear losing clients as a result of being less than impartial in his judgments, did successively alter the existing law to his own advantage.

Moreover, a new level and quality of violence was introduced into society. To be sure, violence had characterized the relationship between men from the beginning of history. But violence, aggression, is costly, and until the development of the institution of a State, an aggressor had to bear the full cost associated with aggression himself. Now, however, with a state-king in place, the costs of aggression could be externalized onto third parties (tax-payers and draftees) and accordingly aggression, or more specifically imperialism, i.e., attempts of aggressively, through war and conquest, enlarging one's territory and one's subject population, increased correspondingly.

Yet how was such a development possible, predictable as its consequences are? While it is not difficult to understand why a feudal king might want to become an absolute king, i.e., the head of a State: for who, except angels, would not like to be in the position where he can decide all conflicts including conflicts involving himself? It is far more difficult to understand how the king, even if he is the most noble of noble people, can get away with such a coup. Obviously, any would-be-State king would run into immediate opposition, most likely and most ferociously from other nobles, since they are the ones who typically own more and have larger estates and hence would have to fear the most from the king's power to tax and legislate.

The answer to this question is actually quite simple and we are essentially familiar with it to this day. The king aligned himself with the "people" or the "common man." He appealed to the always and everywhere popular sentiment of envy among the "underprivileged" against their own "betters" and "superiors," their lords. He offered to free them of their contractual obligations *vis-à-vis* their lords, to make them owners rather than tenants of their holdings, for instance, or to "forgive" their debts to their creditors, and could so corrupt the public sense of justice sufficiently to render the aristocratic resistance against his coup futile. And to console the aristocracy over its loss of power and thus reduce their resistance, the king further offered them posts in his much enlarged and expanded royal courts.

Moreover, to achieve his goal of absolute power the king also aligned himself with the intellectuals. The demand for intellectual services is typically low, and intellectuals, almost congenitally, suffer from a greatly inflated self-image and hence are always prone to and become easily avid promoters of envy. The king offered them a secure position as court intellectuals and they then returned the favor and produced the necessary ideological support for the king's position as absolute ruler. They did this through the creation of a twofold myth: On the one hand they portrayed the history before the arrival of the absolute king in the worst possible light, as a ceaseless struggle of all against all, with one man being another man's wolf — contrary to the actual history of a prior natural aristocratic order. And on the other hand, they portrayed the king's assumption of absolute power as the result of some sort of contractual agreement by his subjects, presumably reached rationally, based on the myth of the otherwise threatening return to the *bellum omnia contra omnes*.

I have already shown that no such contract is conceivable, and that the notion of any such contract is sheer myth. No person in his right mind would sign such a contract. But as I hardly need emphasize, this idea, i.e., that the power of the State as a territorial monopolist of ultimate decision-making is grounded and founded in some sort of contract holds sway in the heads of the populace to this day. Absurd as it is, then, the court intellectuals were remarkably successful in their work.

As the result of the intellectuals' ideological work of promoting this twofold myth: of presenting the rise of absolute monarchs as the result of a *contract*, the king's absolute monarchy was turned into a constitutional monarchy. In schoolbooks and the official, orthodox historiography this transition from absolute to constitutional monarchy is typically presented as a great step forward in human history, as progress. In fact, however, it represented another folly and initiated still further decay. For whereas the position of the absolute king was at best a tenuous one, as the memory of his actual rise to absolute power through an act of usurpation still lingered on and thus effectively limited his "absolute" power, the introduction of a constitution actually formalized and codified his power to tax and to legislate. The constitution was not something that protected the people from the king, but it protected the king from the people. It was a State-constitution, which presupposed what was formerly still considered with greatest suspicion, namely the right to tax without consent and to make laws. The constitutional king, in subjecting himself to a few formalities and procedural routines, was thus enabled to expand his powers and enrich himself far beyond anything possible for him as an absolute monarch.

Ironically, the very forces that elevated the feudal king first to the position of absolute and then of constitutional king: the appeal to egalitarian sentiments and the envy of the common man against his betters and the enlistment of the intellectuals, also helped bring about the king's own downfall and paved the way to another, even greater folly: the transition from monarchy to democracy.

When the king's promises of better and cheaper justice turned out to be empty and the intellectuals were still dissatisfied with their social rank and position, as was to be predicted, the intellectuals turned the same egalitarian sentiments that the king had previously courted in his battle against his aristocratic competitors against the monarchical ruler himself. After all, the king himself was a member of the nobility, and as a result of the exclusion of all other nobles as potential judges, his position had become only more elevated and elitist and his conduct even more arrogant. Accordingly, it appeared only logical that the king, too, should be brought down and that the egalitarian policies which the king had initiated, be carried through to their ultimate conclusion: the control of the judiciary by the common man, which to the intellectuals meant by themselves, as, as they viewed it, the "natural spokesmen of the people."

The intellectual criticism directed against the king was not a criticism of the institution of a legal monopoly of ultimate decision-making, however, which, as I have explained, constitutes the ultimate moral and economic folly and the root of all evil. The critics did not want to return to a natural aristocratic order, in which they themselves would play only a minor albeit important role. But they did, in their criticism, make a superficial appeal to the old and ineradicable notion of the equality of everyone before the law or the superiority of law above all. Thus, they argued that monarchy rested on personal privilege and that such a privilege was incompatible with equality before the law. And they suggested that by opening participation and entry into State government to everyone on equal terms — that is, by replacing a monarchy with a democracy — the principle of the equality of all before the law was satisfied.

Appealing as this argument might at first appear, it is fundamentally wrong, however. Because democratic equality before the law is something entirely different from and incompatible with the old idea of one universal law, equally applicable to everyone, everywhere and at all times. Under democracy, everyone is equal insofar as entry into state government is open to all on equal terms. Everyone can become king, so to say, not only a privileged circle of people, i.e., the king and whomever he in his absolute or constitutional powers designates as his successor. Thus, in a democracy no personal privilege or privileged persons exist. However, functional privileges and privileged functions exist. State agents, i.e., so-called public officials, as long as they act in an official capacity, are governed and protected by public law and occupy thereby a privileged position *vis-à-vis* persons acting under the mere authority of private law.

For one, public officials are, just like any absolute or constitutional king, permitted to finance or subsidize their own activities through taxes. That is, they do not, as every private-law citizen must, earn their income through the production and subsequent sale of goods and services to voluntarily buying or not-buying consumers. Rather, as public officials they are permitted to engage in, and live off, what in private dealings, between private-law subjects, is considered robbery, theft, and stolen loot. Thus, privilege and legal discrimination — and the distinction between rulers and subjects — do not disappear under democracy. To the contrary. Rather than being restricted to princes and nobles, under democracy, privileges come into the reach of everyone: Everyone can participate in theft and live off stolen loot if only he becomes a public official. Likewise, democratically elected parliaments are, just like any absolute or constitutional king, not bound by any superior, natural law, i.e., by law not of their own making (such as and including so-called constitutional law), but they can legislate, i.e., they can make and change laws. Only: While a king legislates in his own favor, under democracy everyone is free to promote and try to put into effect legislation in his own favor, provided only that he finds entry into parliament or government.

Predictably, then, under democratic conditions the tendency of every monopoly of ultimate decision-making to increase the price of justice and to lower its quality is not diminished but aggravated.

Theoretically speaking, the transition from monarchy to democracy involves no more (or less) than the replacement of a permanent, hereditary monopoly "owner" — the king

— by temporary and interchangeable "caretakers" — by presidents, prime ministers, and members of parliament. Both, kings and presidents, will produce "bads," i.e., they tax and they legislate. Yet a king, because he "owns" the monopoly and may sell and bequeath his realm to a successor of his choosing, his heir, will care about the repercussions of his actions on capital values.

As the owner of the capital stock on "his" territory, the king will be comparatively future-oriented. In order to preserve or enhance the value of his property, his exploitation will be comparatively moderate and calculating. In contrast, a temporary and interchangeable democratic caretaker does not own the country, but as long as he is in office he is permitted to use it to his own advantage. He owns its current use but not its capital stock. This does not eliminate exploitation. Instead, it makes exploitation shortsighted, present-oriented, and uncalculating, i.e., carried out with no or little regard for the value of the capital stock. In short, it promotes capital consumption.

Nor is it an advantage of democracy that free entry into every state position exists (whereas under monarchy entry is restricted to the king's discretion). To the contrary, only competition in the production of goods is a good thing. Competition in the production of bads, such as taxation and legislation, is not good. In fact, it is worse than bad. It is sheer evil. Kings, coming into their position by virtue of birth, might be harmless dilettantes or decent men (and if they are "madmen" they will be quickly restrained or, if need be, killed by close relatives concerned with the possessions of the royal family, the dynasty). In sharp contrast, the selection of state rulers by means of popular elections makes it essentially impossible for a harmless or decent person to ever rise to the top. Presidents and prime ministers come into their position not owing to their status as natural aristocrats, as feudal kings once did, i.e., based on the recognition of their economic independence, outstanding professional achievement, morally impeccable personal life, wisdom and superior judgment and taste, but as a result of their capacity as morally uninhibited demagogues. Hence, democracy virtually assures that only dangerous men will rise to the top of state government.

In addition: Under democracy the distinction between the rulers and the ruled becomes blurred. The illusion even arises that the distinction no longer exists: that with democratic government no one is ruled by anyone, but everyone instead rules himself. Accordingly, public resistance against government power is systematically weakened. While exploitation and expropriation — taxation and legislation — before might have appeared plainly oppressive and evil to the public, they seem much less so, mankind being what it is, once anyone can freely enter the ranks of those who are at the receiving end, and consequently there will be more of it.

Worse: Under democracy the social character and personality structure of the entire population will be changed systematically. All of society will be thoroughly politicized. During the monarchical age, the ancient aristocratic order had still remained somewhat intact. Only the king and, indirectly, the members of his (exclusive) court could enrich themselves — by means of taxation and legislation — at other people's and their properties expense. Everyone else had to stand on his own feet, so to say, and owed his position in society, his wealth and his income, to some sort of value-productive efforts. Under democracy, the incentive structure is systematically changed. Egalitarian sentiments and envy are given free reign. Everyone, not just the king, is now allowed to participate in the exploitation — via legislation or taxation — of everyone else. Everyone is free to express any confiscatory demands whatsoever. Nothing, no demand, is off limits. In Bastiat's words, under democracy the State becomes the great fiction by which everyone seeks to live at the expense of everyone else. Every person and his personal property come within reach of and are up for grabs by everyone else.

Under a one-man-one-vote regime, then, a relentless machinery of wealth and income redistribution is set in motion. It must be expected that majorities of have-nots will constantly try to enrich themselves at the expense of minorities of haves. This is not to say that there will be only one class of haves and one class of have-nots, the rich and the poor, and that the redistribution — via taxation and legislation — will occur uniformly from the rich onto the poor. To the contrary. While the redistribution from rich to poor will always play a prominent role and is indeed a permanent feature and mainstay of democracy, it would be naïve to assume that it will be the sole or even the predominant form of redistribution. After all, the rich and the poor are usually rich or poor for a reason. The rich are characteristically bright and industrious, and the poor typically dull, lazy or both. It is not very likely that dullards, even if they make up a majority, will systematically outsmart and enrich themselves at the expense of a minority of bright and energetic individuals. Rather, most redistribution will take place within the group of the non-poor, and it will actually be frequently the better off who succeed in having themselves subsidized by the poor. (Just think of "free" university education, whereby the working class, whose children rarely attend universities, pay for the education of middle-class children!) Indeed, many competing parties and coalitions will try to gain at the expense of others. In addition, there will be a variety of changing criteria defining what it is that makes a person a have (deserving to be looted) and another a have-not (deserving to receive the loot) — and it will be the intellectuals who play a major role in defining and promoting these criteria (making sure, of course, that they themselves will always be classified as have-nots in need of ever more loot). As well, individuals can be members of a multitude of groups of haves or have-nots, losing on account of one characteristic and gaining on account of another, with some individuals ending up net-losers and others net-winners of redistribution.

In any case, however, since it is invariably something valuable, something "good" that is being redistributed — property and income — of which the haves supposedly have too much and the have-nots too little, any redistribution implies that the incentive to beget, have, or produce something of value — something "good" — is systematically reduced and, *mutatis mutandis*, the incentive of not getting, having, or producing anything valuable — of not being or not having anything "good" — but relying instead on and living off redistributed income and wealth is systematically increased. In short, the proportion of good people and good, value-productive activities is reduced and the proportion of bad or not-so-good people and of unproductive habits, character traits, and types of conduct will increase, with the overall result of impoverishing society and making life increasingly unpleasant.

While it is impossible to predict the exact outcome of the permanent democratic struggle of all against all, except to say that it will lead to ever higher taxes, to a never ending flood of legislation and thus increased legal uncertainty, and consequently to an increase in the rate of social time-preference, i.e., increased short-term orientation (an "infantilization" of society), one outcome of this struggle, one result of democracy can be safely predicted, however. Democracy produces and brings about a new power elite or ruling class. Presidents, prime ministers, and the leaders of parliament and political parties are part of this power elite, and I have already talked about them as essentially amoral demagogues. But it would be naïve to assume that they are the most powerful and influential people of all. They are more frequently only the agents and delegates — those doing the bidding — of other people standing on the sidelines and out of public view. The true power elite, which determines and controls who will make it as president, prime minister, party leader, etc., are the plutocrats. The plutocrats, as defined by the great but largely forgotten American sociologist William Graham Sumner, are not simply the super-rich — the big bankers and the captains of big business and industry. Rather, the plutocrats are only a subclass of the super rich. They are those super rich big bankers and businessmen, who have realized the enormous potential of the State as an institution that can tax and legislate for their own even greater future enrichment and who, based on this insight, have decided to throw themselves into politics. They realize that the State can make you far richer than you already are: whether in subsidizing you, in awarding you with state contracts, or in passing laws that protect you from unwelcome competition or competitors, and they decide to use their riches to capture the State and use politics as a means to the end of their own further enrichment (rather than becoming richer solely by economic means, i.e., in better serving voluntarily paying customers of one's products). They do not have to get involved in politics themselves. They have more important and lucrative things to do than wasting their time with everyday politics. But they have the cash and the position to "buy" the typically far less affluent professional politicians, either directly in paying them bribes or indirectly, by agreeing to employ them later on, after their stint in professional politics, as highly paid managers, consultants, or lobbyists, and so manage to decisively influence and determine the course of politics in their own favor. They, the plutocrats, will become the ultimate winners in the constant income and wealth redistribution struggle that is democracy. And in between them (the real power elite staying outside the limelight), and all those whose income (and wealth) depends solely or largely on the State and its taxing power (the employees of the always growing state apparatus and all recipients of transfer payments, its "welfare clients"), the productive middle class gets increasingly squeezed dry.

Not least, democracy has also a profound effect on the conduct of war. I already explained that kings, because they can externalize the cost of their own aggression onto others (via taxes) tend to be more than 'normally' aggressive and warlike. However, a king's motive for war is typically an ownership-inheritance dispute brought on by a complex network of inter-dynastic marriages and the irregular but always recurring extinction of certain dynasties. As violent inheritance disputes, monarchical wars are characterized by limited territorial objectives. They are not ideologically motivated quarrels but disputes over tangible properties. Moreover, as inter-dynastic property disputes, the public considers war essentially the king's private affair to be paid for by himself and as insufficient reason for any further tax increase. Further, as private conflicts between different ruling families the public expects, and the kings feel compelled, to recognize a clear distinction between combatants and non-combatants and to target their war efforts specifically and exclusively against each other and their respective personal properties.

Democracy radically transforms the limited wars of kings into total wars. In blurring the distinction between the rulers and the ruled, democracy strengthens the identification of the public with the State. Once the State is owned by all, as democrats deceivingly propagate, then it is only fair that everyone should fight for their State and all economic resources of the country be mobilized for the State in its wars. And since public officials in charge of a democratic state cannot and do not claim to personally "own" foreign territory (as a king can do), the motive for war instead becomes an ideological one — national glory, democracy, liberty, civilization, humanity. The objectives are intangible and elusive: the victory of ideas, and the unconditional surrender and ideological conversion of the losers (which, because one can never be sure about the sincerity of the conversion, may require the mass murder of civilians). As well, the distinction between combatants and non-combatants becomes fuzzy and ultimately disappears under democracy, and mass war involvement — the draft and popular war rallies — as well as "collateral damage" become part of war strategy.

These tendencies will be still further strengthened by the rise of the new ruling elite of plutocrats. For one, the plutocrats will quickly realize the enormous profits to be made by arming the State, by producing the very weapons and equipment used in war, and in being awarded most generous tax-funded cost-plus contracts to do so. A military-industrial complex will be built up. And second, unlike most people who have merely local or domestic interests, the super-rich plutocrats have financial interests also in foreign places, potentially all around the globe, and in order to promote, protect, and enforce these foreign interests it is only natural for them to use the military power of their own State also to interfere, meddle, or intervene in foreign affairs on their behalf. A business deal in foreign countries may have turned sour or a concession or license may be won there — almost everything can be used as a reason to pressure one's own State to come to their rescue and intervene outside of its own territory. Indeed, even if this intervention requires that a foreign country be destroyed, this can be a boon for them, provided only they receive the contract to rebuild the country that their weapons had before destroyed.

Finally, the tendency already set in motion with the war of kings of leading to increased political centralization, toward the building of empire, is continued and accelerated through democratic war.

Every State must begin territorially small. That makes it easy for productive people to run away to escape its taxation and legislation. Obviously, a State does not like to see its productive people run away and tries to capture them by expanding its territory. The more productive people the State controls, the better off it will be. In this expansionist desire, it runs into opposition by other States. There can be only one monopolist of ultimate decision-making in any given territory. That is, the competition between different States is eliminative. Either *A* wins and controls the territory, or *B*. Who wins? At least in the long run, that State will win — and take over another's territory or establish hegemony over it and force it to pay tribute — that can parasitically draw on a comparatively more productive economy. That is, other things being the same, internally more "liberal" States, i.e., States with comparatively low taxes and little legislative regulation, will win over less "liberal," i.e., more oppressive, States and expand their territory or their range of hegemonic control.

There is only one important element missing still in this reconstruction of the tendency toward imperialism and political centralization: money.

As a territorial monopolist of legislation, every State, whether monarchic or democratic, immediately recognized the immense potential for its own enrichment — far beyond anything offered by taxation — provided by the monopolistic control of money. By appointing itself as the sole producer of money, the State could increase and inflate the money supply through currency depreciation: by producing an increasingly cheaper and ultimately "worthless" money, such as paper money, that could be produced at virtually zero cost, and thus enabled the State to "buy" real, non-monetary goods at no cost to itself. But in an environment of multiple, competing states, paper monies and currency areas, limitations to this policy of "expropriation through inflation" come into play. If one State inflates more than another, its money tends to depreciate in the currency market relative to other monies, and people react to these changes in selling the more inflationary money and buying the less inflationary one. "Better" money would tend to outcompete "worse" money.

This can be prevented only if the inflationary policies of all states are coordinated and an inflation cartel is established. But any such cartel would be unstable. Internal and external economic pressures would tend to burst it. For the cartel to be stable a dominant enforcer is required — which leads back to the subject of imperialism and empire building. Because a militarily dominant State, a hegemon, can and will use its position to institute and enforce a policy of coordinated inflation and of *monetary imperialism*. It will order its vassal States to inflate along with its own inflation. It will further pressure them to accept its own currency as their reserve currency, and ultimately, to replace all other, competing currencies by a single paper money, used worldwide and controlled by itself, so as to expand its exploitative power over other territories and ultimately the entire globe even without further war and conquest.

But — and with that I am slowly approaching the end of my tale of moral and economic folly and decay and have already touched upon a possible way out — imperialism and empire building also bears the seeds of its own destruction. The closer a State comes to the ultimate goal of world domination and one-world government and paper money, the less reason there is to maintain its internal liberalism and do instead what all States are inclined to do anyway, i.e., to crack down and increase their exploitation of whatever productive people are still left. Consequently, with no additional tributaries left and domestic productivity stagnating or falling, the empire's internal policies of bread and circuses and its foreign policies of war and domination can no longer be maintained. Economic crisis hits, and an impending economic meltdown will stimulate decentralizing tendencies, separatist and secessionist movements, and lead to the breakup of empire.

What, then, is the moral of my story? I have tried to make the current world intelligible, to reconstruct it as the predictable result of a series of successive and cumulative moral and economic errors.

We all know the results. The price of justice has risen astronomically. The tax load imposed on property owners and producers makes the burden imposed on slaves and serfs appear moderate in comparison. As well, government debt has risen to breathtaking heights. Everywhere, democratic states are on the verge of bankruptcy. At the same time, the quality of law has steadily deteriorated to the point where the idea of law as a body of universal and immutable principles of justice has disappeared from public opinion and consciousness and been replaced by the idea of law as legislation. Every detail of private life, property, trade, and contract is regulated by increasingly higher mountains of paper laws. In the name of social, public, or national security, democratic caretakers "protect" us from global warming and cooling, the extinction of animals and plants and the depletion of natural resources, from husbands and wives, parents and employers, poverty, disease, disaster, ignorance, prejudice, racism, sexism, homophobia and countless other public "enemies" and "dangers." Yet the only task government was ever supposed to assume — of protecting our life and property — it does not perform. To the contrary, the higher the state expenditures on social, public, and national security have risen, the more private property rights have been eroded, the more property has been expropriated, confiscated, destroyed, and depreciated, and the more have people been deprived of the very foundation of all protection: of personal independence, economic strength, and private wealth. The more paper laws have been produced, the more legal uncertainty and moral hazard has been created, and lawlessness has displaced law and order. And while we have become ever more dependent, helpless, impoverished, threatened and insecure, the ruling elite of politicians and plutocrats has become increasingly richer, more corrupt, dangerously armed, and arrogant.

Likewise, we know about the international scene. The once-upon-a-time comparatively liberal USA, through a seemingly endless series of wars — wars supposed to make the world safe for democracy but in reality wars for US and its plutocrats' world-domination — has risen to the rank of the world's foremost empire and global hegemon, meddling in the domestic affairs and superimposing its rule on countless other countries and their local power elites and populations. Moreover, as the world's dominant empire, the US has also established its currency, the US-dollar as the leading international reserve currency. And with the dollar used as reserve currency by foreign central (government) banks, the US can run a permanent "deficit without tears." That is, the US must not pay for its steady excesses of imports over exports, as it is normal between "equal" partners, in having to ship increasingly more exports abroad (exports paying for imports!). Rather: Instead of using their export earnings to buy American goods for domestic consumption, foreign governments and their central banks, as a sign of their vassal status *vis-à-vis* a dominant US, use their paper dollar reserves to buy up US government bonds to help Americans consume beyond their means at the expense of foreign populations.

What I have tried to show here is why all of this is not a historical accident, but something that was predictable. Not in all details, of course, but as far as the general pattern of development is concerned. That the ultimate error committed, leading to these deplorable results, was the establishment of a territorial monopoly of ultimate decision making, i.e., a State, and hence, that the entire history we are told and taught in schools and standard textbooks, which presents democracy as the crowning achievement of human civilization, is just about the opposite of the truth.

The final question, then, is "Can we rectify this error and go back to a natural aristocratic social order?" I have written and spoken about the ultimate solution: how a modern natural order — a private law society — could and would work, and

I can only summarily refer you here to these works.[3] Instead, I only want to briefly touch here, at the very end, on matters of political strategy: how to possibly approach the ultimate solution that I and others such as my great teacher Murray Rothbard have proposed and outlined — given the current state of affairs.

As indicated, the democratic system is on the verge of economic collapse and bankruptcy as in particular the developments since 2007, with the great and still ongoing financial and economic crisis, have revealed. The EU and the Euro are in fundamental trouble, and so are the US and the US dollar. Indeed, there are ominous signs that the dollar is gradually losing its status as dominant international reserve currency. In this situation, not quite unlike the situation after the collapse of the former Soviet Empire, countless decentralizing, separatist and secessionist movements and tendencies have gained momentum, and I would advocate that as much ideological support as possible be given to these movements.

For even if as a result of such decentralist tendencies new State governments should spring up, whether democratic or otherwise, territorially smaller States and increased political competition will tend to encourage moderation as regards a State's exploitation of productive people. Just look at Liechtenstein, Monaco, Singapore, Hong Kong, and even Switzerland, with its still comparatively powerful small cantons *vis-à-vis* its central government. Ideally, the

[3] I gave a speech at the Mises Institute Brasil in 2011 entitled "The Problem of Social Order." It was published by the Mises Institute in Auburn, Alabama, as "State or Private Law Society," and is available at: mises.org/daily/5270/State-or-PrivateLaw-Society

decentralization should proceed all the way down to the level of individual communities, to free cities and villages as they once existed all over Europe. Just think of the cities of the Hanseatic League, for instance. In any case, even if new little States will emerge there, only in small regions, districts, and communities will the stupidity, arrogance, and corruption of politicians and local plutocrats become almost immediately visible to the public and can possibly be quickly corrected and rectified. And only in very small political units will it also be possible for members of the natural elite, or whatever is left of such an elite, to regain the status of voluntarily acknowledged conflict arbitrators and judges of the peace.

INDEX

abortions, 27
agriculture, 18
  mental skills needed for, 90
animals
  domestication of in history, 58
  extinction of through overhunting, 46n.
  herding of, 52
  husbandry of, 52
  undomesticable, 57
aprioristic laws, 17
argumentation ethics, 10
aristocracy, natural, role of, 109
aristocratic social order, natural, 106
Austrian economics, 15
Austro-Libertarianism, 17

cannibalism, 29
capital accumulation, 73
capital consumption, promotion of, 119
Carthage, 38
children
  parents' obligations toward, 64
  privatization of, 60, 63
Chodorov, Frank, 12
Classical Economics, 15
cognitive development, differential, 35
  collaboration, "selfishly-motivated," 42
commerce between the sexes, 60
comparative advantage, 75
conflict, as solution to overpopulation, 84
conflict resolution
  monopoly on, 104
  need for, 104
  role of the State in, 105
constitution, role of, 116
consumer goods
  indirect and roundabout production of, 54
  production of, 31n., 47
  surplus of, 31n.
contingent empirical events, 16
cooperation
  benefits of, 40
  intra-group, biological basis for, 39

decentralizing tendencies, 131
democracy
  consequences of, 122f.
  effects of on the population, 120
  political privileges under, 118
  political robbery under, 118
  power elites under, 123
  transition to, 116
  wealth redistribution under, 121
democratic legislatures as unbound by natural law, 118
democratic states, current predicament of, 128ff.
diffusion
  cultural, 69
  demic, 69
division of labor, 25, 39, 73, 75, 77
  benefits of, 40f.
domestication
  of dogs
    as private property, 57
  of horses, 58
  wolves, 55f.
    early uses of, 55f.

early interglacial period, 32
egalitarianism, 116
  in social sciences, 100
elected officials, likely personalities of, 119f.
elite, natural, 109
empires
  building of, 126
  the inevitable end of, 128
environment, unappropriated (free goods), 50
envy, promotion of by intellectuals, 114
ethnicities, emergence of, 34
eugenic effects
  negative (dysgenic effects), 101
  positive, 101
evolution, theory of, 76
excess population, solutions to, 27

families, noble, 109
family life, 39
family, 18
  establishment of, 48
  invention of, 59f.
  socialist attitudes to, 61n.
Fertile Crescent, 13
feudal age, natural order of, 110f.
feudalism, allodial, 112
fiat property, 105
Frankfurt school, 9
free goods (environment) vs. economic goods, 49
free love, 62
  and family life contrasted, 65n.
future orientation, 119

Garden of Eden, 103
genetic and linguistic trees of descent, 36n.
global climate, changes in, 37
growing seasons, length of, 95

Habermas, Jürgen, 9
Hanseatic League, 132
hegemon, 127
history, rationally reconstructed, 17
Holocene period, 37
Homo
  Australopithecus, 53
  Erectus, 22, 25, 36, 53
  Ergaster, 22
  Habilis, 21, 53
  Neanderthalensis, 22, 36
  Sapiens, 53
household incomes
  depending on productivity, 64
  differences in, 64f.
human action, universal laws of, 15
human life, physical environment needed for, 91
humans
  archaic, 22
  modern, 24
hunter-gatherer lifestyle
  as supplanted by the Neolithic Revolution, 70
  parasitic nature of, 26, 45
hunter-gatherer societies
  contact between, 34
  division of labor within, 39f.
  effect of technological advances on, 45
  optimal population for, 42n.
  solitary, 21, 40
hunter-gatherers, 21
  antagonistic relations between, 30
  egalitarianism of, 25n.
  expanding land use by, 78
  life expectancy of, 26
  lifestyle of, 25
hunting skills, evolution of, 22

imitation vs. invention, 87
imperialism, 126
  monetary, 127
individual abilities, variations in, 41
Industrial Revolution, 13, 18, 98
  significance of, 82
infanticide, 27
inflation cartel, 127
intellectuals
  court role of, 114
  recruitment of by kings, 114
  role of, 116
intelligence, 18
  as influenced by external conditions, 90
  as influenced by the natural environment, 96
  evolution of among hunter-gatherers, 89
  evolution of, 86ff.
  geographic distribution of, 98
  role of in economic success, 88
  role of in history, 86ff.

judges, monopoly status of, 110
justice, universal principles of, 15

Keeley, Lawrence, 28
kings
  absolute, 14
  absolute, actions of, 112f.
  absolute, aggression by, 113
  as appliers of law, 110
  as judges, 110
  as makers of law, 110
  medieval, role of, 111
knowledge, transmission of, 24
Kuehnelt-Leddihn, Erik von, 11

labor, average product of, 76
land
  appropriation of, 47
  limited availability of, 38
  private ownership of, 18
language
  emergence of, 22
  evolution of, 23
  functions of, 23
  uses for, 23
languages
  proliferation of, 36
  reduction in the number of, 36
Last Glacial Maximum, 37
law of (diminishing) returns, 43f., 76
laws, given vs. discovered, 109
learning, role of language in, 23f.
libertarianism, 16
  cosmopolitan, 17
life-style, nomadic, 25
linguistic differentiation, 35
Little Big Horn, battle of, 29
Little Ice Age, 38n.

Malthus, Thomas R., 60
Malthusian conditions, 13
Malthusian law of population, 44f., 76
Malthusian problem, 46n.
Malthusian trap, 45, 53, 83f., 85, 98
  as described by Mises, 77n.
man
  anatomically modern, 21
  behaviorally modern, 21
Marginal Revolution in economics, 15
Menger, Carl, 15, 49
Middle Ages, 106
migration, 31
  as solution to overpopulation, 84
military superiority, 71
military-industrial complex, rise of, 125
minerals, lack of in tropical soil, 93
Mises, Ludwig von, 9, 15, 30, 50, 76, 84
monarchy
  absolute, 115
  as better than democracy, 11, 118f.
  constitutional, 115
money, political role of, 127

natural order, defined, 112
Neanderthals, 24, 25

Neolithic Revolution, 13, 18, 46n., 47, 78, 98
as intellectual achievement, 53
diffusion of, 69
population expansion possible after, 54n.
Nock, Albert J., 12

objectified arguments, 24
old biological order (agrarian age), 72
one-world government, 128
Oppenheimer, Franz, 12
original appropriation, 104
overhunting, 46
overpopulation, 59
Malthusian consequences of, 83

peaceful life, basis for, 31n.
people, "absolute," 14
per capita incomes, 18
period of production, extended, 97
period of provision, extended, 97
planning horizon, lengthened, 89, 96
plants
cultivation of, 54
domesticated varieties of, 55
plutocrats, 123
popular migrations
due to climate, 32ff.
genetic results of, 34
process of, 34
population control, 73
population density, 27
praxeology, 15, 17
present age, relative wealth of, 106
primitive communism, 48
primitive sexual practices, 61
primitive societies, causes of death in, 28
primitive warfare, nature of, 28
private law, 16
private ownership
establishment of, 104
role of, 104
private property, 25
origin of, 13
privileges, functional, in democracy, 117
procreation
costs and benefits of, 62
incentives of, 62f.
privatization of, 60
production methods, indirect and roundabout, 74
production, non-parasitic mode of, 79
property rights
anarcho-Lockean, 10
private, 84, 85
property
collective, 48
fiat, 105
fiat, defined, 113
nature of, 50
transfer of, 104
prostitution, function of, 68n.
proto-language, human, 35

public officials, privileges of, 117f.

Rawls, John, 107
redistribution
direction of, 121
group warfare under, 122
perverse incentives under, 122
relativism
empirical, 14
ethical, 14
resource limitations as cause of war, 29
revisionist history, 17
Robinson Crusoe, 73
Roman law, 16
Rothbard, Murray, 9, 16, 84
Rousseau's noble savage, 28

Sahul, continent of, 33
saving, 74
savings
plain, 87
productive, 87
Scholastic law, 16
seasonal changes, 94f.
anticipation of, 94
sedentary life, circumstances favorable to, 99
sedentary society, 56
unequal wealth in, 56
serfdom, 112
sexual behavior, moral restraint in, 63
sexuality, socialist attitudes to, 61n.
social conflict
most acceptable solutions to, 107
sources of, 107f.
social contract, 115
sociological studies, 14
sociology, "scientific," 14
specialization, 75
State, the
capture of by plutocrats, 123
functions of, 105
historical development of, 106
origin of, 14
role of under Malthusian conditions, 101
role of under post-Malthusian conditions, 101
stationary society, 77
Stoics, 16

Tahiti, income levels in, 85n.
taxation under feudalism, 111
technological innovation, 77
temperate regions, carrying capacity of, 93
territorial monopoly, 112
time preference, 75, 87
role of in economic success, 88
tools, evolution of, 22
tropical soil, carrying capacity of, 92

UNLV, 10
unowned land, appropriation of, 51f.

wars
conduct of under democracy, 124f.
monarchical, 124
plutocrats' motives for, 125
world per capita income (chart), 82
world population growth (chart), 80
World War I, 28
World War II, 28

ABOUT THE AUTHOR

Hans-Hermann Hoppe was born on September 2, 1949, in Peine, West Germany. He attended the Universität des Saarlandes, Saarbrücken, the Goethe-Universität, Frankfurt/M, and the University of Michigan, Ann Arbor, for studies in Philosophy, Sociology, History, and Economics. He earned his Ph.D. (Philosophy, 1974) and his "Habilitation" (Sociology and Economics, 1981), both from the Goethe-Universität, Frankfurt am Main.

He taught at several German universities as well as at the Johns Hopkins University Bologna Center for Advanced International Studies, Bologna, Italy. In 1985, he moved from Germany to the United States, to study under Murray Rothbard. He remained a close associate of Rothbard until his death in January, 1995.

An Austrian school economist and libertarian/anarcho-capitalist philosopher, he is currently Professor Emeritus of Economics at UNLV, Distinguished Fellow with the Mises Institute, former editor of the *Journal of Libertarian Studies* (1995–2009), and founder and president of The Property and Freedom Society (2006–present).

Professor Hoppe has written extensively, some of his publications include: *Democracy: The God That Failed; The Myth of National Defense; The Economics and Ethics of Private Property; A Theory of Socialism and Capitalism*; *Handeln und Erkennen*; *The Great Fiction; Kritik der kausalwissenschaftlichen Sozialforschung*; *Eigentum, Anarchie und Staat*; *Wettbewerb der Gauner*; and numerous articles on philosophy, economics and the social sciences. His writings have been translated into thirty languages.

He is married to economist Dr. A. Gülçin Imre Hoppe and resides with his wife in Istanbul.

THE MISES INSTITUTE

The Mises Institute, founded in 1982, is a teaching and research center for the study of Austrian economics, libertarian and classical liberal political theory, and peaceful international relations. In support of the school of thought represented by Ludwig von Mises, Murray N. Rothbard, Henry Hazlitt, and F.A. Hayek, we publish books and journals, sponsor student and professional conferences, and provide online education. Mises.org is a vast resource of free material for anyone in the world interested in these ideas.

91596506R00082

Made in the USA
San Bernardino, CA
22 October 2018